Sir **Lewis** Carl Davidson **Hamilton** MBE HonFREng, born in ⬚⬚⬚⬚⬚⬚⬚⬚⬚ Hertfordshire, England, UK on 7th January 1985, is a professional racing driver, who com⬚⬚⬚⬚ previously driven for McLaren from 2007 - 2012. Lewis ha⬚⬚⬚ Championship titles, tied with Michael Schumacher, along⬚ positions (101) & podium finishes (175).

Brought up in Stevenage, Hamilton joined the McLaren y⬚ led to a Formula 1 drive with McLaren in 2007, remaining⬚ Lewis set many records that season as he finished runner⬚⬚ following season, he won his 1st title after overtaking on the last lap of the final race of the season to become the youngest ever F1 World Champion. After 4 more years with McLaren, Hamilton signed with Mercedes during 2013.

Changes to the regulations the following year, mandating the use of turbo-hybrid engines, led to the start of an extremely successful period for Lewis, during which he won 6 more drivers' titles. Consecutive wins came in 2014 then 2015, during an intense rivalry with his team-mate Nico Rosberg. After Rosberg's retirement, Ferrari's Sebastian Vettel became Hamilton's closest rival in a couple of intense championship battles, during which Lewis twice overturned mid-season point deficits to lift successive titles again in 2017 - 2018. His 3rd and 4th consecutive titles followed during 2019 & 2020, equalling Schumacher's record.

Lewis has been credited with increasing the following of Formula 1 worldwide by appealing to a broader audience outside of motor-sport, due to his high-profile lifestyle, environmental and social activism, along with his involvement in music & fashion. He's become prominent in supporting activism to combat racism and push for increased diversity in motor-sport. Hamilton was listed in Time magazine in 2020 as one of the 100 most influential individuals globally then was knighted in the New Year Honours of 2021.

Lewis is of mixed-race, his dad, Anthony Hamilton, being a black man of Grenadian descent, while his mum, Carmen Larbalestier, is white, Lewis having identified as black. His parents separated when he was aged 2, following which he lived with his mother & older half-sisters, Samantha and Nicola, until he was 12. Hamilton then lived with his dad, step-mum, Linda & half-brother Nicolas, who's also a professional racing driver. Lewis was brought up as a Catholic.

His dad bought him a radio-controlled car when he was 5, Hamilton finishing as runner-up in the national BRCA championship the following year, despite competing against adults. Being the only black kid racing at his club, Lewis was subjected to racist abuse. His dad bought him a go-kart for Christmas when he was aged 6, promising to support his racing career as long as he worked hard at school. Anthony took redundancy from his position as an IT manager to support his son, becoming a contractor, sometimes taking up to 4 jobs at a time, including working as a double glazing salesman, dishwasher, and putting up signs for estate agents, while still attending Lewis's races. Anthony later set up his own IT company, while acting as his son's manager until early 2010.

Lewis attended The John Henry Newman School, a voluntary aided Catholic secondary school in Stevenage, where at the age of 5, he took up karate to defend himself from bullying. Hamilton was temporarily excluded when he was wrongly identified as having attacked another pupil who was treated in hospital for their injuries. As well as racing, Lewis played soccer for the school team with Ashley Young, who later became an England international. Hamilton, a fan of Arsenal, said that if Formula 1 hadn't turned out well for him, he would've been a footballer or a cricketer, having played both for his school teams. Lewis enrolled at Cambridge Arts & Sciences (CATS), during February 2001, a private 6th-form college in Cambridge.

Hamilton began karting in 1993, rapidly beginning to win races and cadet class championships. A couple of years later, he became the youngest driver to win the British cadet karting championship at the age of 10 then approached McLaren Formula One team boss Ron Dennis at the Autosport Awards of 1995 for an autograph, saying: "Hi. I'm Lewis Hamilton. I won the British Championship and one day I want to be racing your cars". Ron wrote in his autograph book: "Phone me in 9 years, we'll sort something out then". When Lewis was 12, Ladbrokes took a bet, at 40/1 odds, that he'd win a Formula 1 race before the age of 23; while another predicted, at 150/1 odds, that he'd win the World Drivers' Championship before he was 25. Dennis called Hamilton during 1998, following his 2nd Super One series & British championship wins, to offer him a role in the McLaren driver development programme, including an option of a future F1 seat, making Lewis the youngest driver to get a contract that led to a Formula One drive.

Hamilton continued developing in Intercontinental A (1999), Formula A (2000) and Formula Super A (2001) racing, becoming European Champion in the year 2000 with max pts. In Formula A and Formula Super A, racing for TeamMBM.com, his team-mate was Nico Rosberg, who'd later drive for the Williams & Mercedes teams in Formula 1; the pair teaming up again for Mercedes from 2013 to 2016.

Following his karting triumphs, the British Racing Drivers' Club made Lewis a 'Rising Star' Member during the year 2000. Michael Schumacher made a one-off return to karts in 2001, competing against Hamilton along with other future Formula One drivers Vitantonio Liuzzi and Nico Rosberg. Lewis ended the final in 7th, 4 places behind Schumacher. Although the pair saw little of each other on the track, Michael praised the young Briton:

"He's a quality driver, very strong and only 16. If he keeps this up I'm sure he'll reach F1. It's something special to see a kid of his age out on the circuit. He's clearly got the right racing mentality".

—Michael Schumacher, 2001

Hamilton began his car racing career with the British Formula Renault Winter Series of 2001, finishing 5th, which led to a full Formula Renault UK campaign with Manor Motorsport the following year, in which he came 3rd overall. Lewis remained with Manor for another season, winning the championship ahead of Alex Lloyd, despite missing the last couple of races to make his debut in the season finale of the British Formula 3 Championship. However, in his 1st race he was forced out with a puncture then in the 2nd he crashed out, being taken to hospital after a collision with team-mate Tor Graves.

Asked during 2002 about the prospect of becoming one of the youngest ever F1 drivers, Hamilton replied that his goal was "not to be the youngest in Formula One" but rather "to be experienced then show what I can do in Formula One". He made his debut with Manor in the 2004 Formula 3 Euro Series, ending the year 5th in the championship, having also won the Bahrain F3 Superprix & twice raced in the Macau F3 Grand Prix. Williams had come close to signing Lewis but didn't because BMW, their engine supplier, wouldn't fund him.

Hamilton eventually re-signed with McLaren, whose executive and future CEO Martin Whitmarsh, who was responsible for guiding him through the team's young driver programme, had a "huge row" at the end of the season, with Lewis' dad, Anthony, pushing for him to move up to GP2 for 2005, while Martin thought that he should stay in F3 for a 2nd season, culminating in Whitmarsh tearing up Lewis' contract. However, Lewis called Martin 6 weeks later then re-signed with the team.

Hamilton 1st tested for McLaren during late 2004 at Silverstone then moved to the reigning Euro Series champions ASM for the 2005 season, dominating the championship, winning 15 of the 20 rounds, having also won the Marlboro Masters of Formula 3 at Zandvoort. At the end of the season British magazine Autosport featured him in their 'Top 50 Drivers of 2005' issue, ranking Lewis 24th.

He moved to ASM's sister GP2 team, ART Grand Prix, for the 2006 season, winning the GP2 championship at his first attempt, ahead of Nelson Piquet Jr. & Timo Glock. Hamilton had a dominant win at the Nürburgring, despite a penalty for speeding in the pit lane. During his home race at

Silverstone, he overtook 2 rivals at Becketts, a series of high-speed bends where overtaking is rare. In Istanbul Lewis recovered from a spin that dropped him to 18th place to take 2nd. He won the title in unusual circumstances, getting the final point that he needed after Giorgio Pantano was stripped of fastest lap in the Monza feature race.

Hamilton's victory in the GP2 championship coincided with a vacancy at McLaren following the departure of Juan Pablo Montoya to NASCAR and Kimi Räikkönen to Ferrari. Following months of speculation on whether Lewis, Pedro de la Rosa or Gary Paffett would be paired with defending champion Fernando Alonso for 2007, he was confirmed as the team's 2nd driver. Hamilton was told of McLaren's decision at the end of September, but the news wasn't made public for nearly 2 months, due to concern that it would be overshadowed by the announcement of Michael Schumacher's retirement.

Lewis had his 1st Formula 1 win at the Canadian Grand Prix of 2007, only his 6th Grand Prix. In his 1st season in F1 he partnered 2-time & defending World Champion Fernando Alonso, being the only black driver to have raced in the series. After finishing on the podium in his debut, Hamilton went on to set several records as he finished runner-up in the World Drivers' Championship of 2007 to Kimi Räikkönen by a point, including that of the most consecutive podium finishes from debut (9), the joint most wins in a debut season (4) and the most points in a debut season (109). During the season, Lewis & Alonso were involved in a number of incidents which led to tension between both drivers and the team, culminating in Alonso & McLaren terminating their contract by mutual consent in November. Following a successful first season at McLaren, Hamilton signed a £multi-million contract to stay with the team until 2012.

Lewis' success continued in 2008, with 5 victories and 10 podium finishes but he was accused of arrogance & dangerous driving, although he argued that his self-belief was wrongly interpreted and that his driving was firm but fair. As the season reached its finale in Brazil, it became a clear 2-way fight for the title between the home favourite Felipe Massa and Hamilton, who won his 1st title in dramatic fashion, overtaking Timo Glock for 5th position on the final corners of the last lap to become the youngest Formula One World Champion in history, denying race-winner Massa the title by a point. Lewis was the 1st British driver to win the F1 World Championship since Damon Hill during 1996.

During his last 4 years with McLaren, Hamilton continued to have podium finishes & race victories, having entered the final round of the 2010 season with a chance of winning the title, but finishing 4th as Sebastian Vettel won the race to take his 1st drivers' crown. 2011 was the first season that he'd been beaten by a team-mate, as Jenson Button was the runner-up to champion Vettel, during a year in which distractions in his private life and run-ins with FIA (Fédération Internationale d'Automobile) officials led to Lewis finishing 5th, after which he vowed that he'd return to form in 2012. Hamilton had 4 race-wins during that season, to come 4th at its conclusion, surprisingly announcing before the end of the year that he'd be joining Mercedes for 2013, replacing the retiring Michael Schumacher.

Upon signing with Mercedes, Lewis was reunited with his childhood karting team-mate, Nico Rosberg, some pundits describing the move to a team with no recent history of success, as a big gamble. In his 1st season with the Silver Arrows, Hamilton had only one race victory, at the Hungarian Grand Prix, where he converted an unexpected pole position into a winning margin of over 11 secs ahead of Kimi Räikkönen, alongside a number of podium finishes & pole positions, finishing 4th again, for the 3rd time in 5 years.

Changes to regulations for the season of 2014, which mandated the use of turbo-hybrid engines, contributed to the beginning of a highly successful era for Lewis. During that year Mercedes won 16 of the 19 races, 11 of those by Hamilton who came out on top in a season-long duel for the title with team-mate Rosberg. Clinching his 2nd drivers' title, eclipsing the victory total of all previous British drivers, Lewis declared over team-radio after the final race in Abu Dhabi: "This is the greatest day of my life".

New driver number regulations brought in for 2014 allowed drivers to pick an unique car number to use for their entire career, so Hamilton decided to drive under his old karting No. 44 for the rest of his career. Before the start of the season of 2015, Lewis announced that he'd not be switching his car number to 1, as was allowed by reigning world champions, instead continuing to race as No. 44. It was the 1st season since 1994, when Alain Prost retired from the sport after lifting his 4th World Drivers' Championship title the previous year, that the field didn't have a car with the No. 1.

Hamilton dominated the 2015 season, winning 10 races and finishing on the podium a record 17 times as he matched his hero Ayrton Senna's 3 World Championships titles. The rivalry between him & Rosberg intensified, climaxing in a heated battle at the US Grand Prix where Lewis won in an action-packed, wheel-to-wheel battle with his team-mate to clinch the title with 3 races to spare. That year he extended his contract with Mercedes for 3 more years in a deal worth over £100 million, making him one of the best-paid F1 drivers, as well as allowing Hamilton to retain his own image rights, unusual in the sport, and keep his championship-winning cars & trophies.

Lewis' engine failure in Malaysia during 2016 was a key moment in the Drivers' Championship. Despite having more pole positions and race wins than any other driver that season, he lost the drivers' title by 5 pts to his team-mate, Nico. The team's policy of letting the pair compete freely led to several acrimonious exchanges both on & off the track, culminating in Hamilton defying team-orders at the season finale in Abu Dhabi by deliberately slowing to back Rosberg into the chasing pack at the end of the race, in an unsuccessful attempt to encourage other drivers to overtake his team-mate, which would've allowed him to win the title. A succession of poor starts from Lewis early in the season, along with the crucial engine blow-out in Malaysia led to Nico lifting the title, before announcing his shock retirement from the sport immediately after his triumph.

Following Rosberg's retirement, Ferrari's Sebastian Vettel became Hamilton's closest rival as the pair swapped the championship lead throughout 2017 in a tense title contest. Lewis had 11 pole positions that season, breaking the record for the all-time most pole positions, and his consistency, finishing every race in the points, as well as the lack of a serious challenge from his new team-mate Valtteri Bottas, led to him taking 9 race victories while lifting his 4th World Drivers' title, as he overturned a points deficit to Vettel in the 1st half of the season, before clinching the title in Mexico with a couple of races to spare.

The season of 2018 was the 1st time that a couple of 4-time World Champions, Hamilton & Vettel, competed for a 5th title, being labelled the 'Fight for 5' by journalists and fans. As during the previous year, Ferrari & Sebastian seemed to have the upper hand for much of the season, staying ahead until the half-way point. However, Vettel's season unravelled due to a number of driver errors & mechanical problems, while Lewis' run of 6 wins from 7 in the latter half of the season led to him clinching the title in Mexico for the 2nd year running, as he set a new record for the most points scored in a season (408). He signed a 2-year contract with Mercedes during the season, worth up to £40 million / year, making him the best-paid Formula One driver in history.

Hamilton led the drivers' standings for most of the 2019 season, fending off title challenges from team-mate Bottas, the Honda-powered Red Bull of Verstappen and Ferrari's recently promoted Leclerc, to clinch his 6th drivers' title at the United States Grand Prix with 2 races remaining. Lewis ended the season with 11 wins, matching his previous best of 2014 & 2018, along with 17 podiums, matching the all-time record for a 4th time, as well as having 5 pole positions. His total of 413 pts for the season was a new all-time record, Hamilton finishing 87 pts ahead of runner-up Valtteri.

He won his 7th drivers' title in 2020, equalling Michael Schumacher's record, during a season strongly affected by the COVID-19 pandemic. Lewis had 11 wins over the shortened 17-race season, including one in Portugal to break Schumacher's record of 91 wins. He also had 14 podium places and 10 pole positions. Hamilton missed that year's Sakhir Grand Prix after contracting COVID-19, the first race he'd missed since his debut during 2007. He clinched the title at the Turkish Grand Prix with 3 races to spare, ending the season 124 pts clear of his team-mate, runner-up Bottas.

During F1's We Race as One campaign & growing global support for the Black Lives Matter movement, Lewis took the knee ahead of every race he entered and wore t-shirts with the Black Lives Matter slogan. Hamilton and Valtteri's W11 cars were also given a black livery, as a statement of Mercedes' commitment to diversity. He signed a contract to continue racing for the team that year in February 2021. Lewis became the 1st driver to reach 100 pole positions in Formula One at the Spanish Grand Prix that May then during July he signed a contract to remain with Mercedes until the end of 2023.

Hamilton is considered to be one of the most complete drivers on the grid, excelling over a wide range of areas, having an aggressive driving style, with a natural aptitude for identifying the limits of the car. Mark Hughes, wrote on the official Formula 1 website that Lewis is 'super-hard on the brakes ... but has a fantastic ability to match how quickly the down-force is bleeding off with his modulation of the pressure, so that there's no wasted grip but no locked wheels either'.

Paddy Lowe, former engineering director for McLaren, observed that Hamilton is comfortable with levels of rear instability that most other drivers would find intolerable. He's also been praised for his ability to adapt to variances in car set-up & changing track conditions; throughout his career Lewis has usually used less fuel than his team-mates, due to his ability to carry momentum through corners despite instability in the car. Pedro de la Rosa, a former test driver for McLaren who worked with Hamilton and Alonso, rated the pair as the best that he'd seen, stating that they shared a strength in terms of 'how much speed they can run into the apex of a corner while still having a decent exit speed', highlighting their ability to maintain that speed when their rear tyres have lost grip over a longer period.

Lewis has been praised for his consistency, particularly during his time at Mercedes, having finished 33 successive races in point-scoring positions from 2017 to 2018, a run which only ended due to mechanical issues rather than driver error. Ross Brawn wrote that 'over the course of 2018 Hamilton hardly put a foot wrong, winning not only the races he should have, but also some where the opposition was stronger, which is the true mark of a champion'. Ahead of the season of 2021, Martin Brundle, commentating for Sky Sports, said 'I think what has stood out about Lewis over the years is how few mistakes he makes, how complete he is & clean ... he just never makes a mistake in wheel-to-wheel combat or in qualifying ... He just doesn't fade, mentally or physically'.

Hamilton is considered to be one of the best wet-weather drivers in the sport, giving some of his best performances in those conditions. At the British Grand Prix of 2008 he beat runner-up Nick Heidfeld by over a minute, the largest margin of victory since the Australian Grand Prix of 1995. During the turbo-hybrid era, Lewis was unbeaten in every race affected by wet weather from the Japanese Grand Prix of 2014 up to the German Grand Prix of 2019 , when his near 5-year streak was broken by Max Verstappen.

His wet weather drive at the Turkish Grand Prix of 2020, when he clinched his 7th world title was widely praised, with Joe Saward describing it as 'one of his greatest performances': Despite only qualifying 6th for the race after Mercedes struggled with tyre temperatures and a track that lacked grip after being recently resurfaced, during the race he gambled on a 1-stop strategy in mixed conditions, whilst his rivals chose to change their tyres for a 2nd time, allowing him to take the lead then win by over 30 secs. Hamilton's performance was contrasted with that of his team-mate Valtteri Bottas, who spun 4 times before finishing a lap behind in 14th place. Lewis cited the race as his 'stand-out' performance of that season.

Ayrton Senna was a major influence on his driving style, Hamilton stating: 'I think it's partly because I watched him when I was young & I thought 'This is how I want to drive when I get the opportunity' then I went out there and tried it on the kart track. My whole approach to racing has developed from there'. He's been compared to Senna in raw speed. Lewis drove Senna's original title-winning McLaren MP4/4 during 2010, as part of a tribute documentary by the BBC2 motoring show Top Gear, in which he named Senna as the # 1 driver ever, as did several fellow racing drivers.

Hamilton was criticised for being hot-headed at times early in his career, as when he was disqualified in Imola during the GP2 Series of 2006 for overtaking the safety car, which he repeated 4 years later in Formula One at the European Grand Prix of 2010 in Valencia. Lewis was credited with demonstrating greater maturity after his move to Mercedes, while maintaining his ruthlessness & aggression. The official F1 website describes him as 'invariably a fierce but fair fighter'.

'As a driver he's absolutely outstanding – as good as there's ever been. Apart from the talent, he's a good guy, he gets out on the street to support and promote Formula 1. He's box office, 100%'.

—Bernie Ecclestone, 2015

Hamilton has been described as the best driver of his generation & one of the greatest Formula One drivers. Several F1 drivers and experts have described him as the greatest Formula 1 driver of all time. Jim Holden writing in Autocar suggested that Lewis might not only be among the greatest British drivers in Formula One, but one of the greatest British sportsmen. Despite the plaudits from experts & fans in and out of the sport, Hamilton has been seen as a divisive figure in the eyes of the general public, with some journalists arguing that his exploits on the track have been under-appreciated.

Holden has suggested that racial bias might have contributed towards Lewis' perceived lack of popularity relative to his achievements, with his mixed-race & physical appearance – often wearing earrings, dreadlocks and designer clothing – alienating some of the sport's traditional white, elderly male fan-base. Others have attributed the lack of appreciation to the predictability of results during the turbo-hybrid era, likening his period of dominance to that of Michael Schumacher in the early 2000s & to tennis players Steffi Graf and Martina Navratilova, all of whom became more appreciated during the latter part of their careers.

'What strikes me about him now is his maturity ... Hamilton recognises that he's a role model & the influence he has and the responsibilities that come with it. He is far broader than purely a driver in Formula One. He has opinions about the environment, young folk, fashion & music. That's part of the greater appeal of Lewis today'.

—David Richards, chairman of Motorsport UK, 2019

Hamilton's jet-set lifestyle and interests outside Formula 1 have been discussed. He's been praised for disregarding convention & public opinion and described as one of the last superstar drivers. Between race weekends Lewis has travelled around the world several times to explore a variety of interests, as during 2018, when after winning the Italian Grand Prix, he flew to Shanghai and New York where he released his own designer clothing line with Tommy Hilfiger, before flying on to win the next race in Singapore. Toto Wolff has been vocal in his support for Hamilton's off-track pursuits, stating that freedom allows him to perform at his best.

Emerson Fittipaldi & Christian Horner are among those who've supported Lewis' ability to connect with fans, Bernie Ecclestone having also often expressed his admiration of Hamilton's ability to promote the sport, observing that he's happy to engage with fans, unlike some of his peers. Since his rookie season of 2007, Formula One's annual global revenue had risen by 53%, to $1.83 billion by 31st July 2016. Sports journalist for The Telegraph, Luke Slater, stated that 'there have been few better representatives of the sport than Hamilton ... both on and off the track'. Following Lewis' knighthood in 2020, newly appointed F1 CEO Stefano Domenicali said that Hamilton 'is a true giant of our sport' & that 'his influence is huge, both in and out of a car'.

'He was able to win with a dominant car, with a good car like 2010 or 2012, or with bad cars like 2009 & 2011. Not all the champions can say that'.

—Fernando Alonso, 2017

A prodigious talent as a teenager, Lewis established himself as one of the world's best drivers following his record-breaking rookie year. Paddy Lowe stated that 'he turned out to be the best rookie that there's ever been' and that 'his 1st half-season was just the most extraordinary in history'.

After his 1st world title Sebastian a year later, many folk regarded Hamilton as the best driver of his generation. Following Red Bull & Vettel's 4-year dominance of the sport, Lewis' resolve was tested both professionally and personally, as he didn't finish higher than 4th in the Drivers' Championship from 2009 to 2013, leading some to question whether he was the best driver in the sport. Despite this, Hamilton's less successful years with McLaren have also been cited as a demonstration of driving ability as he's won at least one race for 14 successive seasons, attracting high praise from experts & fellow drivers for producing race-winning performances from cars that weren't dominant.

After Lewis clinched his 2nd and 3rd World Championship titles with Mercedes during 2014 & 2015, David Coulthard declared that he was the best driver of his generation, calling him 'the Ayrton Senna of his era', an opinion that was widely accepted among the public, experts, and fellow & former drivers. As Hamilton came to be regarded as the best driver of his era, public and expert debate moved from his status in modern Formula One to that among the greatest drivers in history.

Over the next few seasons Lewis broke a number of records, including that of the most pole positions of all-time, ahead of Michael Schumacher, leading him to be regarded by many as the greatest qualifier in history. After winning his 4th & 5th world titles, Hamilton's place among the greats of the sport became well established in the opinions of experts, rivals and team-mates alike, with some journalists & pundits regarding him as the greatest Formula 1 driver of all time.

After Lewis clinched a 6th World Drivers' Championship title in 2019, ex-Formula One driver Johnny Herbert acclaimed him as the greatest driver ever, an opinion echoed by his Mercedes team-boss Toto Wolff, who described him as 'maybe the best driver that has ever existed', while F1 staff writer, Greg Stuart, described Hamilton as 'arguably the most complete Formula 1 driver ever'. Following his 7th title during 2020, John Watson stated that he 'is, by a million miles, the greatest driver of his generation and you can argue that he'll go on to be the greatest Formula One driver of all time', highlighting Lewis' fearlessness as being key to his success, as evidenced by his performance against double world champion team-mate Alonso in his rookie season & his decision to leave McLaren for Mercedes. Herbert compared him to tennis player Roger Federer and golfer Tiger Woods. After Hamilton's win at the Turkish Grand Prix of 2020, which secured his 7th title, fellow podium finishers Sebastian Vettel & Sergio Pérez both acclaimed him as the greatest driver of their generation.

Lewis' helmet throughout his karting years was predominantly yellow with blue, green and red ribbons. In later years a white ring was added & the ribbons were moved forward to make room for logos and adverts. He continued to have a mainly yellow design for the early stage of his Formula 1 career, but in 2014 decided to change to mostly white, choosing his helmet design from fan submissions. The winning design used a white & yellow base colour with red and orange details & the addition of 3 stars, one for each of Hamilton's 3 F1 championships, on either side. Over the following seasons he added more stars to his helmet, upon winning further World Championship titles.

Lewis has worn specially designed one-off helmets on several weekends throughout his career. At the Monaco Grand Prix of 2010, he had an altered helmet design with a roulette wheel image on the top. At the Malaysian Grand Prix of 2015, Hamilton brought with him a striking blue-&-green design in honour of team sponsor Petronas but wasn't allowed to wear the helmet by the FIA. Hamilton has worn gold coloured helmets 3 times. After winning his 4th title during 2017, he entered that year's Abu Dhabi Grand Prix in a gold helmet with 4 stars adorning the top, with the words World Champion. Lewis donned a gold helmet at the following season's Abu Dhabi Grand Prix after sealing his 5th world title, which was referred to by 5 stars on either side of the design then at the Abu Dhabi Grand Prix of 2019 wore one with 6 stars, following his 6th World Championship title.

Hamilton has also used one-off helmet designs to pay tribute to influential figures in his career, having worn a special helmet in tribute to Ayrton Senna at the Brazilian Grand Prix of 2011, which was auctioned after the race in aid of the Ayrton Senna Foundation. At the Monaco Grand Prix of 2019, Lewis, along with fellow driver Sebastian Vettel, wore a special helmet to pay tribute to Niki Lauda, who'd passed away at the start of the week. The helmet was painted red and white, Lauda's classic colours & had his name printed on the back.

After the race, Hamilton reflected on Niki's career, saying: 'Ultimately, as a driver, my goal one day is to hopefully be as respected as he was ... He's definitely someone who led by a great example, left a great example, and was a real hero to so many'. Lewis again wore a special helmet to pay tribute to Ayrton Senna at the Brazilian Grand Prix of 2019.

In Hamilton's debut season he was partnered by 2-time & defending World Champion Fernando Alonso, with tensions developing between the pair and McLaren due to several incidents, the 1st emerging after Lewis finished runner-up to Fernando at Monaco in 2007. Following post-race comments made by Hamilton suggesting that he'd been forced into a supporting role, the FIA investigated whether McLaren had broken rules by enforcing team orders. They denied favouring Alonso, with the FIA subsequently vindicating them, stating that 'McLaren were able to pursue an optimum team strategy because they had a substantial advantage over all other cars ... nothing which could be described as interfering with the race result'.

Tensions surfaced again at the Hungarian Grand Prix, where during the final qualifying session Lewis went out on the track ahead of Fernando, ignoring requests from the team to let him through: the 2 drivers had been taking turns on a race-by-race basis to lead during qualifying, which gave the leading driver an edge due to the fuel load regulations then in place, with Alonso having been due to lead in Hungary. Hamilton was then delayed in the pits by Fernando, so was unable to set a final lap time before the end of the session.

Fernando was relegated to 6th place on the starting grid, thus promoting Hamilton, who'd qualified 2nd, to 1st, while McLaren was docked Constructors' Championship points. Lewis said that he thought the penalty was 'quite light if anything', only regretting the loss of points. Hamilton was reported to have sworn at Dennis on the team radio following the incident. British motorsport journal Autosport stated that this 'led Dennis to throw his headphones on the pit wall in disgust: a gesture that was misinterpreted by many to be in reaction to Alonso's pole'. However, McLaren later issued a statement on behalf of Lewis denying the use of any profanity.

Due to the events of the 2007 season, the relationship between Lewis & Fernando broke down, with the pair not on speaking terms for a while. In the aftermath it was said that Hamilton had been targeted by Luca di Montezemolo to drive for Ferrari during 2008. The rivalry between the pair led to speculation that either Lewis or Alonso would leave McLaren at the end of the season; Fernando and McLaren terminating their contract by mutual consent in November of that year, ending the pair's time as team-mates.

In later years, tensions between the two dissipated, being replaced by mutual respect, with Alonso praising Hamilton during 2017, saying "Lewis was able to win with a dominant car, with a good car like 2010 or 2012, or with bad cars like 2009 & 2011. Not all the champions can say that". Fernando later described Hamilton as one of the top 5 greatest drivers of all time. On the cool-down lap after Alonso's final race before his 2-year break in 2018, Lewis joined Vettel in paying tribute to Fernando by driving, each on one side, in a formation to the start-finish straight where all 3 executed donuts.

In their time together as team-mates, Hamilton and Alonso won 8 of 17 races in the Formula One season of 2007. Lewis had 4 victories, 12 podium finishes & qualified ahead of Fernando 10 times. Alonso also had 4 victories, 12 podium finishes but qualified ahead of Hamilton only 7 times. At the end of their season as team-mates, the pair were tied on 109 pts, with Lewis coming 2nd and Fernando 3rd in the World Drivers' Championship by virtue of Hamilton having more runners-up finishes.

When Lewis joined Mercedes in 2013, he was paired alongside old karting team-mate & friend Nico Rosberg. Over their 4 seasons as team-mates, a period of Mercedes dominance of F1, the pair's relationship became strained, at times leading to volatile confrontations on and off the track. Hamilton and Rosberg were first team-mates during the year 2000, when they were still in karting.

They raced for Mercedes Benz McLaren in Formula A, where Lewis became European champion, with Nico not far behind. Robert Kubica, who raced with them before Formula 1, recalled that they were competitive both on & off the track, saying that 'They'd even have races to eat pizza, always eating 2 at a time'. Sports journalist Paul Weaver contrasted their upbringings; Rosberg, an only child, was born in Germany but brought up in Monaco, being the son of wealthy former Formula One world champion, Keke Rosberg, whereas Hamilton was born on a council estate in Stevenage, with his dad having to work several jobs to fund his son's junior racing.

Pundit and commentator Will Buxton compared the character & driving styles of the pair, assessing Lewis as the faster driver with more natural ability but with an intellect to match Nico's. Buxton wrote: 'Man to man against Rosberg, I can't recall a single race this year where in the same machinery Hamilton's fuel usage has been higher. He's made his tyres last. He's had to fight from the back of the field time and again (think Germany, think Hungary), yet he hasn't overworked his tyres, he hasn't used too much fuel. He's learned how to drive these new cars & to extract the most from them using the least ... Far from the unintelligent chancer many paint Lewis to be, he's proving to be the intellectual match of his team-mate and the better racer to boot'.

Their old karting boss, Dino Chiesa, said Hamilton was the faster driver whereas Nico, who once said to Chiesa 'everything relates to physics & maths', was always more analytical. This led some to believe that Rosberg would have greater success in Formula 1, the highest level of open-wheel racing, due to the intellectual capacity required to manage brakes, energy harvesting, tyre management and moderate fuel usage. However, Lewis' tyre management often allowed him to push on for longer, enabling optimum race strategies, with his fuel usage regularly being better than almost anyone on the grid.

Sky Sport's Mark Hughes, said: 'Nico has a more scientific methodology, looking to fine-tune more specifically than Hamilton, who typically tends just to find a balance he can work with then adapt his driving around it'. During their time together as team-mates, Lewis & Rosberg won 54 of 78 races over 4 seasons. Hamilton had 32 victories, 55 podium finishes and qualified ahead of Nico 42 times. Rosberg had 22 victories, 50 podium finishes & qualified ahead of Hamilton 36 times. During this period, Lewis won 2 World Championship titles to Nico's 1, and scored more points in 3 out of their 4 seasons together.

Hamilton stated that his rivalry with Sebastian Vettel was his favourite, believing that their battles helped bring them closer together. After 3 years of Mercedes' dominance from 2014 to 2016, Ferrari produced a car that was capable of competing for the championship in 2017 & 2018. Sebastian, who was then driving for Ferrari, had an early lead on points, but Mercedes and Lewis fought back to win the championship in both seasons. Although there were some on-track flash points, including at the Azerbaijan Grand Prix of 2017, when Vettel accused Hamilton of brake checking, driving into him in retaliation, getting a penalty, the pair developed a strong mutual respect in a hard but fairly contested rivalry. Lewis recalled during 2021:

'Mine and Seb's battle was my favourite so far. It's knowing that I was racing against an incredible driver, not only that but a great man in Seb, who's a 4-time world champion & we were racing against another team - he was at Ferrari who were very strong. It took a lot out of both of us during that period of time, to remain focused to deliver weekend in, weekend out. That was a difficult period for us but it brought us closer, because the respect we have between us is huge'.

The only black driver to have raced in F1, Hamilton has been subjected to racist abuse throughout his career, including from Spanish Formula One supporters at the Chinese Grand Prix of 2007. Lewis was heckled and otherwise abused during pre-season testing the following year at the Circuit de Catalunya by several Spanish spectators who wore black face paint, black wigs & shirts bearing the words 'Hamilton's family'. The FIA warned Spanish authorities about the repetition of such behaviour and launched a 'Race Against Racism' campaign.

Shortly before the Brazilian Grand Prix of 2008, a website owned by the Spanish branch of the New York-based advertising agency TBWA, named pinchalaruedadeHamilton, which translates as 'burst Hamilton's tyre', was exposed in the British media. The site contained an image of Interlagos that allowed users to leave nails & porcupines on the track for Lewis' car to run over. Among thousands of comments left since 2007, some included racial insults. Hamilton was subjected to on-line racist abuse in 2021 following a dramatic win at the British Grand Prix. Mercedes, Formula One and the FIA, issued a joint statement condemning the abuse, calling for those responsible to be held accountable.

Lewis' treatment by the media & critics has been criticised for being racist. The Guardian journalist Joseph Harker highlighted double-standards in his treatment compared to other British drivers by British newspapers during 2014, suggesting that his skin colour was a factor in a perceived lack of acceptance by the British public. Footballer Rio Ferdinand in 2019 described media scrutiny of Hamilton as having 'racist undertones', contrasting his treatment with that of fellow British driver Jenson Button.

At the start of his Formula One career, Lewis said that he 'tried to ignore the fact that I was the 1st black guy ever to race in the sport' but later stated that he'd since begun to 'appreciate the implications', having changed his approach to promote equality within the sport. Toto Wolff, his team boss at Mercedes, stated during 2019 that Hamilton was 'scarred for life' by racist abuse inflicted during his childhood.

"People come up to me from different ethnic backgrounds saying, 'My kid wants to be you one day', and I can assure you that when I started racing, there weren't folk from those. I take great pride in that'.

—Lewis Hamilton 2017

Lewis is a prominent advocate against racism & for increased diversity in motor-sport, having questioned racial politics in Formula 1 on several occasions. After being summoned to see the stewards in 5 out of the first 6 races of the season of 2011, Hamilton said, 'Maybe it's because I'm black, that's what Ali G says'. He criticised the lack of diversity in F1 in 2018, stating that nothing had changed during his 11 years in the sport before saying: 'Kids, people, there are so many jobs in this sport of which anybody, no matter your ethnicity or background, can make it and fit in'.

Lewis took the knee before every race that he entered during the Formula One season of 2020 in support of the Black Lives Matter movement, having worn t-shirts bearing the Black Lives Matter slogan. Following the murder of George Floyd by US police while being arrested during May that year, which led to global protests, Hamilton criticised prominent figures in Formula 1 for their silence on the issue, writing on Instagram:

'I see those of you who're staying silent, some of you the biggest of stars, yet you stay silent in the midst of injustice. Not a sign from anybody in my industry, which of course is a white dominated sport. I'm one of the only folk of colour there, yet I stand alone. ... I would have thought by now that you'd see why this happens then say something about it but you can't stand alongside us. Just know that I know who you are & I see you. ...

I don't stand with those looting and burning buildings but those who're protesting peacefully. There can be no peace until our so called leaders make change. This isn't just the US, this is the UK, this is Spain, this is Italy & all over. ... The way minorities are treated has to change, how you educate those in your country of equality, racism, classism and that we're all the same. We're not born with racism & hate in our hearts, it's taught by those we look up to'.

Following Lewis' comments, several drivers released statements about George Floyd's death, voicing their support for the Black Lives Matter movement, with support being expressed by other figures in the sport including Toto Wolff, the Mercedes team boss. Ross Brawn, managing director of F1, said that the organisation 'supports Hamilton totally', describing him as 'a great ambassador for the sport'.

Ross thought Lewis' comments 'are very valid' and that the sport 'can give greater opportunity for minority & ethnic groups to get involved in motor-sport'. Brawn stated that Formula One was working to increase diversity within the sport, with efforts being targeted at increasing driving opportunities at grass-roots level, as well as across all roles in Formula 1.

During the Tuscan Grand Prix weekend of 2020, including on the podium, Hamilton wore a T-shirt with the demand 'Arrest the cops who killed Breonna Taylor' on the front and 'Say her name' with a photo of Taylor on the back. Following an investigation, the FIA announced that only race suits done up to the neck could be worn on the podium & that only official team attire could be worn in the media pen. In anticipation of the FIA's decision, Lewis said that he recognised that they had 'certain limits that they feel that they have to work within', but that he didn't 'regret a single moment of it', citing the 'really positive ... support ... from the fans'.

It was announced during June 2020 that he'd established The Hamilton Commission with the Royal Academy of Engineering, which had been in development since December 2019 but was publicly launched to coincide with the heightened media and public interest in the Black Lives Matter movement & greater scrutiny of racial inequality in society. The partnership with the Royal Academy of Engineering was established to find ways in which motor-sport could engage more young folk from black backgrounds with science, technology, engineering and mathematical subjects then employ them in motor-sport & other engineering sectors.

Lewis became the 1st recipient of the inaugural Laureus Athlete Advocate of the Year Award in May 2021 for his involvement in the fight against racism. Building on the recommendations of the Hamilton Commission, he launched Mission 44 during July 2021, a charitable foundation created to help young folk from under-represented backgrounds achieve their ambitions in wider society. Lewis pledged £20m of his own money to support the work of the charity, including supporting organisations and programmes that narrow the gap in employment & education. Mission 44 work in conjunction with a joint charitable foundation between Hamilton and the Mercedes F1 team, named Ignite, which was also launched in July 2021. Ignite focuses on increasing diversity in motor-sport, by improving educational opportunities & offering financial support.

Lewis confronted Bahrain's human rights abuses during December 2020 and spoke out on allegations of sports-washing. He said that he 'won't let it go unnoticed' after an 11-year-old boy, Ahmed Ramadhan, wrote a letter to Hamilton, asking him to save his dad, who was facing the death penalty, after a confession was allegedly extracted through torture over the death of a policeman. Lewis spoke to human rights organisations, legal experts & Bahraini officials about the country's human rights. The Formula One champion said that although he had no authority to choose the locations of his races, 'going to these countries and just ignoring what's happening in those places' isn't the right way.

Hamilton donated US$500,000 in January 2020 to fire services & animal welfare charities helping with the bushfire crisis in Australia. He's an advocate for animal rights, often using his social media platform to inform fans about issues affecting animals. Lewis has often discussed environmental issues on social media, at conferences, in interviews and documentaries. He asked Mercedes-Benz to remove leather from the company's models worldwide during 2019 : 'I'm trying to push for sustainability with my team. I'm trying to get more involved in Formula One & be more conscious. Mercedes-Benz is a huge organisation. I've got a phone call with the CEO later today to discuss how we can work on getting rid of all the leather supplied to the cars. That's something I want to be involved in'.

Hamilton announced in 2020 that he was aiming to be carbon neutral by the end of that year, saying: 'I don't allow anyone in my office, but also within my household, to buy any plastics. I want everything recyclable, down to deodorant, down to toothbrushes, all these kinds of things ... I'm trying to make as much change as I can in my personal space. I sold my plane over a year ago. I fly a lot less now. I'm trying to fly less through the year'.

Lewis' Neat Burger restaurant donated free meals to front-line NHS workers in 2020, during the COVID-19 pandemic. Neat Burger also launched the 'Kids Eat Free' scheme, serving free meals to school children during the half-term break. Hamilton became the 1st ambassador for the Invictus Games Foundation in 2015, supporting wounded, injured, and sick servicemen & women. He became a Global Education Ambassador for Save the Children during 2013, supporting and promoting its education campaigns.

Lewis began working with the United Nations Children's Fund (UNICEF) in 2012, travelling to the Philippines that March, where he made a short film about Manila's street children, which was shown on ITV1 during Soccer Aid, helping to raise over £4.9 million for UNICEF. While in India for the Grand Prix that October, Hamilton visited a UNICEF-funded newborn care unit & nutrition centre, saying: 'As a sportsman in the public eye, I know I have a role to play in helping to tell the stories of the world's most vulnerable children and I jumped at the chance to be able to do that again after a visit to Manila'.

Lewis travelled to Haiti during 2014, where he made a short film about child malnutrition, which was shown on ITV1 during Soccer Aid, helping to raise over £6 million for UNICEF. He took part in an exhibition to highlight UNICEF's work the following year & to celebrate its 20-year partnership with Starwood Hotels. Hamilton joined the Super Dads initiative in June 2017, a special UNICEF campaign that highlighted the critical role played by fathers in early childhood development. He visited Havana with UNICEF that August to learn more about its 1st development programmes in Cuba.

Lewis partnered with charity campaign #TOGETHERBAND during 2020, to help promote the United Nations' 17 Global Goals. As part of his campaign work, he visited Alperton Community School in North West London to speak to the pupils about the importance of education. Hamilton is a GOAL 4 Ambassador, focusing on the fight to provide quality education to all children. He's also involved in charitable work through the creation of the Lewis Hamilton Foundation, registered in June 2008, which provides grants and donations to charitable causes.

Over the past decade he's made time for other good causes, including making hospital visits to sick children. Lewis has invited fans, young folk & their families to join him at Grand Prix races and social events. He often donates personal & professional paraphernalia for charity auctions, having auctioned a racing kart, raising over £42,000 for baby charity Tommy's. Hamilton raised £6,411 for the Small Steps Project during 2018, £6,000 the following year then another £4,000 for it in 2020, while a donated race suit raised €20,000 for vulnerable children. He often attends charitable functions, having supported projects and charities including the Make-A-Wish Foundation, Comic Relief, Rays of Sunshine, Children in Need & Stevenage's Keech Hospice Care Children's Service.

Lewis controversially shared a video on Instagram of his nephew wearing a princess dress in December 2017, saying: 'Why did you ask for a princess dress for Christmas, boys don't wear princess dresses'. He was condemned for this on social media and by LGBT charities then deleted the video before deleting all content from his social media channels, although he returned to actively using his social media accounts on 17th January 2018. Hamilton apologised for his comments, later appearing at Disneyland Paris with his nephew, who wore a princess dress for the trip, as well as featuring on the front cover of GQ wearing a rainbow tartan kilt that he designed with Tommy Hilfiger, saying: 'I've done something then realised the effect I've had ... I want to make amends. I accept it, realise it & I'm glad that I'm accountable for it'.

Lewis caused controversy at the BBC Sports Personality of the Year Awards during December 2018, when he said on live TV, 'It really was a dream for us all as a family to do something different. For us to get out of the slums', before adding, 'Well, not the slums, but to get out of somewhere and do something. We all set our goals very, very high but we did it as a team'. The leader of Stevenage Borough Council described his comments as 'disappointing', saying that folk felt 'very offended'.

Hamilton posted a video on Instagram in which he apologised for his comments, stating 'I'm super proud of where I come from & I hope you know that I represent in the best way I can always ... Particularly when you're up in front of a crowd, trying to find the right words to express the long journey you've had in life, I chose the wrong words'. The town mayor later accepted his 'gracious apology'.

Lewis has been recognised regularly in the Powerlist, an annual ranking of influential Black Britons, in which he came in the top 10 in 2016 then 2017. He was named the most influential Black Briton in the 14th Powerlist during 2021, for his sporting success and his advocacy in the Black Lives Matter movement. Hamilton was listed as one of Time magazine's 100 most influential people globally in 2020 then was knighted in the New Year Honours of 2021 for services to motor-sports.

He was one of several figures whose tax arrangements were singled out in a report by the charity Christian Aid during 2008, having received criticism from British members of parliament that year for avoiding UK taxes. Following the leak of the Paradise Papers in November 2017, it was reported that Lewis had avoided paying £3.3 million of VAT on his private jet, worth £16.5 million. BBC Panorama stated that the leasing deal set up by his advisers was 'artificial' & 'didn't comply with an EU and UK ban on VAT refunds for private use'.

The BBC program also stated that Hamilton's Instagram account provided evidence that the jet was used for personal trips. The jet was sold during September 2019. Despite not residing in the UK, HMRC data published that year, put him among the top 5,000 highest UK tax payers. Lewis told The Sunday Times in 2014: 'What folk don't realise is that I pay tax here in the UK, but I don't earn all my money here. I race in 19 different countries, so I earn my money in 20 different places and I pay tax in several different places & I pay a lot here as well. I'm contributing to the country'.

Hamilton also has interests in music, saying that 'music has been a huge passion of mine since I was really young. I started playing guitar when I was 13. In here, I can be me, I can be vulnerable. I can show a side of me that folk don't get to see'. He featured on Christina Aguilera's song 'Pipe' [2018] under the pseudonym XNDA, but he didn't confirm this until July 2020, when he revealed that he'd been writing and recording music for 10 years. Lewis featured in the movie Cars 2, in which he voiced an anthropomorphic version of himself then a voice command assistant in Cars 3, used by Cruz Ramirez. He was credited as an executive producer of the documentary film The Game Changers [2018].

Hamilton launched the clothing line TOMMYXLEWIS that year during New York Fashion Week with American fashion designer Tommy Hilfiger, alongside models Winnie Harlow & Hailey Baldwin. He stated 'Growing up, I remember seeing the iconic Tommy Hilfiger flag', while Hilfiger said 'Lewis is bold in everything he does ... He's not afraid to take risks and he has a cool & sophisticated style that really speaks to the new generation of Tommy fans'. Daily Front Row listed him during August 2020 as one of a group of high-profile investors who bought W, a troubled fashion magazine. The following month he launched X44 to compete in the all-electric SUV off-road racing series Extreme E, from the 2021 season onwards.

Hamilton launched a vegan restaurant named Neat Burger during September 2019, as the first international plant-based burger chain. Neat Burger was crowned Best Vegan Restaurant of the Year in 2020, at the Deliveroo Restaurant Awards. Lewis told the BBC during 2017 that he'd gone vegan because 'as the human race, what we're doing to the world ... the pollution coming from the amount of cows that are being produced is incredible. The cruelty is horrible and I don't necessarily want to support that & I want to live a healthier life'. The following year Hamilton was named the PETA Person of the Year for his vegan activism. He said in 2018 that he'd given up drinking 'a while ago'.

Lewis is a fan of art, one of his favourite artists being Andy Warhol, having worn a gold-framed version of Warhol's Cars, Mercedes-Benz 300 SL Coupe painting hanging from a chain around his neck before the United States Grand Prix of 2014. Hamilton was in an on/off relationship with Nicole Scherzinger from November 2007 to February 2015, lead singer of the American girl group Pussycat Dolls. He owns 2 1967 AC Cobras, 1 black, 1 red, and in February 2015, he bought a LaFerrari from 'his rivals in Maranello'.

Lewis was suspended from driving in France for a month on 18th December 2007 after being caught speeding at 122 mph on a French motorway in a Mercedes-Benz CLK, which was impounded. A couple of days before the Australian Grand Prix of 2010, Victoria Police saw him 'celiberately losing traction' in his silver Mercedes-AMG C63, impounding the car for 48 hrs, with Hamilton releasing a statement of apology for 'driving in an over-exuberant manner'. After being charged with intentionally losing control of a vehicle, he was fined A$500, being described as a 'hoon' by the magistrate.

Lewis moved to Luins, Vaud canton, Switzerland during 2007, saying that his main reason for leaving the UK was for privacy, later stating on the TV show Parkinson that taxation was also a factor. Along with many other Formula 1 drivers he moved to Monaco in 2010, buying a house for £10 million, also owning an apartment in Manhattan, New York, which he bought for US$40 million in 2017 & an estate in Colorado where he's said that he'll live after his retirement.

Hamilton was ranked as the richest British sports-person during 2015, with an est mated personal fortune of £88 million, which increased to a net worth of £159 million by 2018 then £224 million by 2020, making him the richest British sports star in the history of the Sunday Times Rich List. Lewis signed a contract to stay with Mercedes until the end of the 2018 season before the Monaco Grand Prix weekend of 2015, in a deal worth more than £100 million over the 3 years, making him one of the best-paid F1 drivers. In the week leading up to the German Grand Prix of 2018, Hamilton signed a 2-year contract with Mercedes, worth up to £40 million / year, making him the best-paid driver in the history of Formula One.

Racing record

Karting career summary

Season	Series	Team	Position
1995	Super 1 National Championship – IAME Cadet		1st
1996	Kartmasters British Grand Prix – Comer Cadet		1st
1997	Super 1 National Championship – Formula Yamaha		1st
1998	Torneo Industrie – 100 Junior		19th
	Green Helmet Trophy – Cadets		12th
	Italian Open Masters – ICA Junior		4th
1999	Torneo Industrie Open – ICA		1st
	South Garda Winter Cup – ICA Junior		6th
	Trofeo Andrea Margutti – 100 Junior		18th
	Italian Open Masters – ICA Junior		4th
	European Championship – ICA Junior		2nd
2000	Trofeo Andrea Margutti – Formula A		7th
	World Cup – Formula A	MBM.com	1st
	European Championship – Formula A		1st
	World Championship – Formula A		20th
2001	South Garda Winter Cup – Formula Super A		7th
	Italian Open Masters – Formula A	MBM.com	4th
	World Championship – Formula Super A		15th

Racing career summary

Season	Series	Team	Races	Wins	Poles	F/Laps	Podiums	Points	Position
2001	Formula Renault UK Winter Series	Manor Motor-sport	4	0	0	0	0	48	7th
2002	Formula Renault UK	Manor Motor-sport	13	3	3	5	7	274	3rd
	Formula Renault 2000 Eurocup		4	1	1	2	3	92	5th
2003	Formula Renault UK	Manor Motor-sport	15	10	11	9	13	419	1st
	British Formula 3 Championship		2	0	0	0	0	0	NC
	Formula Renault 2000 Masters		2	0	0	0	1	24	12th
	Formula Renault 2000 Germany		2	0	0	0	0	25	27th
	Korea Super Prix		1	0	1	0	0	N/A	NC
	Macau Grand Prix		1	0	0	0	0	N/A	NC
2004	Formula 3 Euro Series	Manor Motor-sport	20	1	1	2	5	69	5th
	Bahrain Superprix		1	1	0	0	1	N/A	1st
	Macau Grand Prix		1	0	1	0	0	N/A	14th
	Masters of Formula 3		1	0	0	0	0	N/A	7th
2005	Formula 3 Euro Series	ASM Formule 3	20	15	13	10	17	172	1st
	Masters of Formula 3		1	1	1	1	1	N/A	1st
2006	GP2 Series	ART Grand Prix	21	5	1	7	14	114	1st
2007	Formula One	Vodafone McLaren Mercedes	17	4	6	2	12	109	2nd
2008	Formula One	Vodafone McLaren Mercedes	18	5	7	1	10	98	1st
2009	Formula One	Vodafone McLaren Mercedes	17	2	4	0	5	49	5th
2010	Formula One	Vodafone McLaren Mercedes	19	3	1	5	9	240	4th
2011	Formula One	Vodafone McLaren Mercedes	19	3	1	3	6	227	5th
2012	Formula One	Vodafone McLaren Mercedes	20	4	7	1	7	190	4th
2013	Formula One	Mercedes AMG Petronas F1 Team	19	1	5	1	5	189	4th
2014	Formula One	Mercedes AMG Petronas F1 Team	19	11	7	7	16	384	1st
2015	Formula One	Mercedes AMG Petronas F1 Team	19	10	11	8	17	381	1st

Year	Formula One	Team					
2016	Formula One 380	Mercedes AMG Petronas F1 Team	21	10	12	3	17
	2nd						
2017	Formula One 13 363	Mercedes AMG Petronas Motor-sport 1st		20	9	11	7
2018	Formula One 17 408	Mercedes AMG Petronas Motor-sport 1st		21	11	11	3
2019	Formula One 17 413	Mercedes AMG Petronas Motor-sport 1st		21	11	5	6
2020	Formula One 347 1st	Mercedes-AMG Petronas F1 Team	16	11	10	6	14
2021	Formula One 221.5* 2nd*	Mercedes-AMG Petronas F1 Team	13	4	3	4	10

* Season still in progress.

Complete Macau Grand Prix results

Year	Team	Car	Qualifying	Quali Race	Main race
2003	United Kingdom Manor Motor-sport	Dallara F303	18th	N/A	DNF
2004	United Kingdom Manor Motor-sport	Dallara F304	2nd	1st	14th

Complete Formula 3 Euro Series results

Year	Entrant	Chassis	Engine								
1	2	3	4	5	6	7	8	9	10	11	12
	13	14	15	16	17	18	19	20	DC	Points	

2004   Manor Motor-sport   Dallara F302/049 HWA-Mercedes

HOC 1 11	HOC 2 6	EST 1 Ret	EST 2 9	ADR 1 Ret	ADR 2 5
PAU 1 4	PAU 2 7	NOR 1 1	NOR 2 3	MAG 1 Ret	MAG 2 21
NÜR 1 3	NÜR 2 4	ZAN 1 3	ZAN 2 6	BRN 1 7	BRN 2 4
HOC 1 2	HOC 2 6	5th 68			

2005   ASM Formule 3   Dallara F305/021 Mercedes

HOC 1 1	HOC 2 3	PAU 1 1	PAU 2 1	SPA 1 DSQ	SPA 2 1
MON 1 1	MON 2 1	OSC 1 3	OSC 2 1	NOR 1 1	NOR 2 1
NÜR 1 12	NÜR 2 1	ZAN 1 Ret	ZAN 2 1	LAU 1 1	LAU 2 1
HOC 1 1	HOC 2 1	1st 172			

Complete GP2 Series results

Year	Entrant										
1	2	3	4	5	6	7	8	9	10	11	12
	13	14	15	16	17	18	19	20	21	DC	Points

2006   ART Grand Prix   VAL

FEA 2 VAL SPR 6   IMO FEA DSQ IMO SPR 10   NÜR FEA 1   NÜR SPR 1
CAT FEA 2   CAT SPR 4   MON FEA 1   SIL FEA 1   SIL SPR 1
MAG FEA 19   MAG SPR 5   HOC FEA 2   HOC SPR 3   HUN FEA 10   HUN SPR 2
IST FEA 2   IST SPR 2   MNZ FEA 3   MNZ SPR 2   1st   114

Complete Formula One results

Year   Entrant Chassis Engine

1	2	3	4	5	6	7	8	9	10	11	12
13	14	15	16	17	18	19	20	21	22	WDC	Points

2007   Vodafone McLaren Mercedes   McLaren MP4-22 Mercedes FO 108T 2.4 V8

AUS 3 MAL 2 BHR 2 ESP 2 MON 2 CAN 1 USA 1 FRA 3 GBR 3 EUR 9 HUN 1
    TUR 5   ITA 2   BEL 4   JPN 1   CHN Ret   BRA 7   2nd   109

2008   Vodafone McLaren Mercedes   McLaren MP4-23 Mercedes FO 108V 2.4 V8

AUS 1 MAL 5 BHR 13 ESP 3 TUR 2 MON 1 CAN Ret FRA 10 GBR 1 GER 1 HUN 5
EUR 2 BEL 3 ITA 7 SIN 3 JPN 12 CHN 1 BRA 5   1st   98

2009   Vodafone McLaren Mercedes   McLaren MP4-24 Mercedes FO 108W 2.4 V8

AUS DSQ MAL 7‡ CHN 6 BHR 4   ESP 9 MON 12 TUR 13 GBR 16 GER 18 HUN 1
    EUR 2   BEL Ret   ITA 12†   SIN 1   JPN 3   BRA 3 ABU Ret   5th   49

2010   Vodafone McLaren Mercedes   McLaren MP4-25 Mercedes FO 108X 2.4 V8

BHR 3 AUS 6 MAL 6 CHN 2 ESP 14† MON 5 TUR 1 CAN 1 EUR 2 GBR 2 GER 4
HUN Ret BEL 1 ITA Ret SIN Ret   JPN 5   KOR 2 BRA 4 ABU 2   4th   240

2011   Vodafone McLaren Mercedes   McLaren MP4-26 Mercedes FO 108Y 2.4 V8

AUS 2 MAL 8 CHN 1 TUR 4 ESP 2   MON 6   CAN Ret EUR 4 GBR 4 GER 1 HUN 4
BEL Ret   ITA 4   SIN 5   JPN 5 KOR 2   IND 7   ABU 1 BRA Ret   5th   227

2012   Vodafone McLaren Mercedes   McLaren MP4-27 Mercedes FO 108Z 2.4 V8

AUS 3 MAL 3   CHN 3 BHR 8 ESP 8   MON 5   CAN 1 EUR 19†   GBR 8   GER Ret
HUN 1   BEL Ret   ITA 1   SIN Ret   JPN 5   KOR 10   IND 4   ABU Ret   USA 1 BRA Ret
        4th   190

2013   Mercedes AMG Petronas F1 Team Mercedes F1 W04   Mercedes FO 108F 2.4 V8

AUS 5   MAL 3 CHN 3 BHR 5 ESP 12 MON 4 CAN 3 GBR 4 GER 5 HUN 1 BEL 3 ITA 9
SIN 5 KOR 5 JPN Ret IND 6 ABU 7 USA 4 BRA 9   4th   189

2014   Mercedes AMG Petronas F1 Team Mercedes F1 W05 Hybrid Mercedes PU106A Hybrid 1.6
V6 t

AUS Ret   MAL 1 BHR 1 CHN 1 ESP 1 MON 2 CAN Ret AUT 2 GBR 1 GER 3 HUN 3
BEL Ret   ITA 1 SIN 1 JPN 1 RUS 1 USA 1 BRA 2 ABU 1   1st   384

2015   Mercedes AMG Petronas F1 Team Mercedes F1 W06 Hybrid Mercedes PU106B Hybrid 1.6 V6 t

AUS 1	MAL 2	CHN 1	BHR 1	ESP 2	MON 3	CAN 1	AUT 2	GBR 1	HUN 6	BEL 1		
ITA 1	SIN Ret	JPN 1	RUS 1	USA 1	MEX 2	BRA 2	ABU 2				1st	381

2016   Mercedes AMG Petronas F1 Team Mercedes F1 W07 Hybrid Mercedes PU106C Hybrid 1.6 V6 t

AUS 2	BHR 3	CHN 7	RUS 2	ESP Ret	MON 1	CAN 1	EUR 5	AUT 1	GBR 1	HUN 1		
GER 1	BEL 3	ITA 2	SIN 3	MAL Ret	JPN 3	USA 1	MEX 1	BRA 1	ABU 1			
	2nd	380										

2017   Mercedes AMG Petronas Motor-sport   Mercedes AMG F1 W08 EQ Power+Mercedes M08 EQ Power+ 1.6 V6 t

AUS 2	CHN 1	BHR 2	RUS 4	ESP 1	MON 7	CAN 1	AZE 5	AUT 4	GBR 1	HUN 4		
BEL 1	ITA 1	SIN 1	MAL 2	JPN 1	USA 1	MEX 9	BRA 4	ABU 2			1st	363

2018   Mercedes AMG Petronas Motor-sport   Mercedes AMG F1 W09 EQ Power+Mercedes M09 EQ Power+ 1.6 V6 t

AUS 2	BHR 3	CHN 4	AZE 1	ESP 1	MON 3	CAN 5	FRA 1	AUT Ret	GBR 2	GER 1		
HUN 1	BEL 2	ITA 1	SIN 1	RUS 1	JPN 1	USA 3	MEX 4	BRA 1	ABU 1		1st	408

2019   Mercedes AMG Petronas Motor-sport   Mercedes AMG F1 W10 EQ Power+Mercedes M10 EQ Power+ 1.6 V6 t

AUS 2	BHR 1	CHN 1	AZE 2	ESP 1	MON 1	CAN 1	FRA 1	AUT 5	GBR 1	GER 9		
HUN 1	BEL 2	ITA 3	SIN 4	RUS 1	JPN 3	MEX 1	USA 2	BRA 7	ABU 1		1st	413

2020   Mercedes-AMG Petronas F1 Team Mercedes AMG F1 W11 EQ Performance   Mercedes M11 EQ Performance 1.6 V6 t

AUT 4	STY 1	HUN 1	GBR 1	70A 2	ESP 1	BEL 1	ITA 7	TUS 1	RUS 3	EIF 1	POR 1	
EMI 1	TUR 1	BHR 1	SKH	ABU 3							1st	347

2021   Mercedes-AMG Petronas F1 Team Mercedes AMG F1 W12 EQ Performance   Mercedes M12 E Performance 1.6 V6 t

BHR 1	EMI 2	POR 1	ESP 1	MON 7	AZE 15	FRA 2	STY 2	AUT 4	GBR 12	HUN 2		
BEL 3‡	NED 2	ITA	RUS	TUR	USA	MXC	SAP	SAU	ABU			
2nd*	221.5*											

† Did not finish, but was classified as he'd completed over 90% of the race distance.
‡ Half points awarded as less than 75% of race distance was completed.
* Season still in progress.

Formula One records

Lewis debuted at the Australian Grand Prix of 2007, becoming the 1st black driver in Formula One. He has the most career wins, most pole positions, most podium finishes, most career points, and most laps led. When Hamilton won the F1 World Championship of 2008, after finishing 5th in the Brazilian Grand Prix, he became the youngest ever driver to win the championship at the age of 23 years, 301 days, a record that was beaten by Sebastian Vettel in 2010.

Honours and achievements

Formula 1

Formula One World Drivers' Championship: 2008, 2014, 2015, 2017, 2018, 2019, 2020

Formula One World Constructors' Championship: 2014, 2015, 2016, 2017, 2018, 2019, 2020

DHL Fastest Lap Award: 2014, 2015, 2017, 2019, 2020

FIA Pole Trophy/Pirelli Pole Position Award: 2015, 2016, 2017, 2018, 2020

Hawthorn Memorial Trophy: 2007, 2008, 2012, 2013, 2014, 2015, 2016, 2017, 2018, 2019

Lorenzo Bandini Trophy: 2009

Other awards

Lewis won the Laureus Breakthrough of the Year Award during 2008 then the Sportsman of the Year Award in 2020. He also won the Pride of Britain Awards (2007), Best Driver ESPY Award (2017), BBC Sports Personality of the Year Award (2014; 2020), L'Équipe Champion of Champions (2020) & Gazzetta World Sportsman of the Year (2018; 2020). Hamilton was elected FIA Personality of the Year 3 times (2014; 2018; 2020), having been inducted into FIA Hall of Fame during 2017.

Orders and special awards

Member of the Order of the British Empire

Knight Bachelor

Honorary Award, Grenada

Recognition

A portrait of Lewis by photographer Dario Mitidieri is displayed in the National Portrait Gallery, London.

The Hamilton Straight, Silverstone Circuit.

A Vodafone McLaren Mercedes press attaché set up a standard interview backdrop of 3 panels festooned with logos in the paddock at the Canadian Grand Prix at 3:30 p.m. one Friday. Within minutes a couple of dozen TV cameramen had assembled in front of it despite the fact that the man they hoped to film, Lewis Hamilton, wasn't due to arrive for another hour. They stood vigil because, at that moment in the world of motor-sport, there'd have been no greater calamity than for the 22-yr-old British driver to materialize with no minicam present to record the moment for posterity.

The attaché reappeared 20 mins later assuring those present that a 4:30 pm appearance was still expected, mercifully authorizing the press to get out of the afternoon sun. That's how it was with Lewis in those days: folk gathered for the possibility. With a front-running drive to his 1st Grand Prix victory that Sunday in Montreal, Hamilton moved to the top of the drivers' standings in only the 6th race of his Formula 1 career, leapfrogging his McLaren team-mate, defending world champion Fernando Alonso. Lewis was heading for the U.S. Grand Prix in Indianapolis that weekend, off to the best start of any rookie in F1 history.

As he took his 1st pass of the circuits, Hamilton was also making a series of figurative left-hand turns into traffic. Being Formula One's 1st black driver was the least of it, Willy T. Ribbs having test-driven a car for Brabham in 1986, but never actually raced. Lewis was a babe in a sport that rarely treated youth kindly, also being a Brit driving for McLaren, a whiskered name in British motor-sport that had last won a Formula 1 team title during 1998. Thus, Hamilton was playing out multiple roles as the Great Black, Young, British Hope.

Of those 3 mantles, race may've been the easiest to bear. Formula 1 had been able to draft in the slipstream of inevitable comparisons with Tiger Woods, another out-riding prodigy who brought new fans to a largely white sport. Anthony Hamilton had played the role of Earl Woods, the doting dad who, recognizing a knack & a passion in his son, made sacrifices for the sake of the boy's development. The son of Grenadian immigrants, Anthony had once held down 3 jobs so young Lewis Carl, named after the US athlete Carl Lewis, could race go-karts.

Hamilton junior shared Tiger's self-possession and steady temper, despite earning a living amidst ear-splitting noise & hot tarmacadam, not hushed galleries and lush fairways. Like Woods, he also had a piebald racial background, his mum, Carmen, who split from Anthony when Lewis was aged 2, being white, while Tiger wasn't more precocious than Lewis, who at the age of 6 had already appeared on a BBC kid's show, Blue Peter, to demonstrate his talent at racing remote-controlled cars that his dad had assembled for him.

Hamilton still raced those cars with his 16-yr-old half-brother, Nicholas, who had cerebral palsy. Lewis graduated from the remote a couple of years later, after discovering karts during a family holiday in Spain. At an awards banquet in December 1995, wearing a borrowed black tie, the 10-yr-old Lewis -- by then Britain's youngest-ever Cadet Class Karting Champion -- famously walked up to McLaren chief Ron Dennis to ask for an autograph, telling him, "I want to race for you one day". "Phone me in 9 years," Hamilton recalled Dennis replying. "Confidence, devoid of all arrogance, is the best way to describe Lewis' approach to me that night", said Ron.

Less than 3 years later, he made Hamilton the youngest driver ever to land a F1 contract, signing him up as an apprentice in McLaren's young driver development program, so Anthony no longer had to moonlight to support his son's career. Lewis progressed rapidly after that: World No 1 ranking in Formula A Karting during the year 2000, again being the youngest ever; the British Formula Renault title in '03 then championships in Formula One's Double A and Triple A circuits, Euro F3 & GP2, in '05 and '06. The pressure wouldn't get to him on the F1 circuit, Hamilton Jnr. having stated that March, because "I control it & filter it", as if he'd long ago been fitted with something from a car parts store.

By signing Alonso then giving Lewis its # 2 car for the 2007 season, McLaren was facing challenges of its own making, albeit problems that almost any racing team would love to have had. During the pre-season McLaren executive Martin Whitmarsh had sketched out 'an ideal scenario', in which Fernando, 25, lifted another world championship title, while Hamilton was groomed as the driver to take the team into the future. Although fine in theory, reality had set in a fortnight earlier in Monaco.

With Alonso and Lewis running 1st-2nd late in the race, McLaren radioed Hamilton to make a pit stop. Several British journalists inferred from the rookie's post-race comments that Lewis, who finished 2nd, was upset that he hadn't been allowed to go after the win. The tabloids became so indignant that they briefly suspended their investigation of Hamilton's love life - 'Lewis Gave Me Grand Prix on the Back Seat of His Mini' The News of the World had trumpeted late that May - to howl over the injustice of it all.

However, wiser heads in the motoring press had challenged Fleet Street's presumption. On Monte Carlo's perilous circuit, with a No. 1, world champion driver having taken pole, holding a lead, it wouldn't have been sensible to risk a crash that could've wiped out both winner & runner-up, but the outcry, along with Ron's statement that his drivers had been instructed to "hold station" over the final laps - "You virtually have to decide in advance which 1 of the team's 2 drivers will claim the victory", he said - raised enough suspicion for the the Fédération Internationale d'Automobile to jump in. After rabbinically parsing the difference between midst-of-race 'team orders' (forbidden) and overarching 'team strategy' (allowed), the FIA pronounced that McLaren had permissibly practised the latter. That was one place where Hamilton parted company with Woods: No 3rd party had ever stymied a back-9 hole charge against Duval, Els & Mickelson.

If he hadn't been a rookie, who was so preternaturally competitive, Lewis would've better hidden his disappointment in front of the press in Monte Carlo. By the time he'd reached Montreal the previous week, he'd been more carefully on message. "The team's going to give me an equal opportunity" to win the championship. "I need to remember that I'm extremely privileged to be part of such a fantastic team. They want to see me win as much as I want to win. I'm only 5 races into my Formula 1 career. As team the boss has choices to make", he'd said that Thursday.

However, Hamilton had also shown a streak of defiance: "Maybe next time I might watch what I say, but I just said what I felt. I'm only human. Sometimes your feelings need to be expressed. You can't always just put a big smile on your face. Every weekend, when I'm matching Fernando's times, I do as well if not better. I'm demonstrating that I can be world champion. I'd hate to be in the situation Rubens was in. If that was the case, I wouldn't be here much longer", he'd said, referring to Rubens Barrichello, who'd led almost the entire Austrian Grand Prix of 2002, only to let Michael Schumacher - for long cast as Johnny Carson to Barrichello's Ed McMahon - slip past him 100m from the finish-line, at Ferrari's direction -- prompting the FIA to formally ban 'team orders'.

After Lewis beat his team-mate while finishing 2nd in Alonso's home race, the Spanish Grand Prix, on May 13th '07, the British weekly magazine Autosport ran a headline hinting at 'civil war', so Fernando might've been concerned that McLaren would favour the British driver who'd been Dennis' protégé of long standing. However, team personnel described a professional bonhomie, with the pair engaging in good-natured bouts of NBA PlayStation in the team trailer. "We're committed to creating an environment where both can excel. It's difficult at the moment. In some instances, the media don't want the sporting answer. They want the human-interest answer. Right now, we're in a no-win situation", said Ron, who in over almost 3 decades had never before entrusted a McLaren car to a rookie. Finish 1-2, but find yourself in a no-win situation.

Niki Lauda had once called men who were drawn to the cockpit of a Formula One car to indulge the need for speed 'Wankers. Any joy is from fascination with perfection, not from a thrill of driving fast'. If that was true, surely Hamilton would've been relishing the season, regardless of his record. In his fastidiousness, his eagerness to sponge up all he could from the over 1,000 individuals marshalled in his support, and his usual imperturbability, he seemed uncommonly well-equipped to pursue the perfect race. Until that week, Lewis had never driven Montreal's Circuit Gilles Villeneuve, yet he grabbed the first pole position of his F1 career in Saturday's qualifying. Afterwards, asked if he found the feeling to be better than sex, he considered the question then replied "You know what? I'd say it is better than sex".

By qualifying 1st, Hamilton could've spent that Sunday chasing perfection by outrunning imperfection all around him. Fernando missed the 1st turn of the race, nearly clipping Lewis while re-entering the track from a run-out. 4 times the yellow flag came out, once after a crash that sent BMW Sauber's Robert Kubica pin-balling from barrier to barrier, before being taken by helicopter to hospital, where doctors declared him to be in stable condition & conscious with a broken leg. Almost half of the 22 drivers failed to finish, including 2 who were black-flagged for running a red light when leaving the pits.

"That was lots of go-karting experience there. You get that in karting, and you've got to keep your head straight", Anthony Hamilton said afterwards. What his dad called keeping your head straight & his mentor described as "confidence, devoid of arrogance", was a kind of balance that hinted at perfection, Dennis having known it to be there for a dozen years. That weekend someone asked the

McLaren boss if anything about Lewis' rookie season so far had surprised him. "The only thing that's surprised me, is that Lewis would put sex after pole position", said Ron.

'When I first started in Formula One, I tried to ignore the fact that I was the 1st black guy ever to race in the sport, but as I've got older, I've really started to appreciate the implications. It's a pretty cool feeling to be the person to knock down a barrier - just like the Williams sisters did in tennis or Tiger Woods in golf. I get kids from all different cultures and nationalities coming up to me now, all wanting to be F1 drivers. They feel that the sport is open to everyone. That's why it was so great to do the Top Gear festival in Barbados last weekend.

I had so much fun, although being there meant so much more to me than having a good time. My immediate family are from the West Indies - from Trinidad and Grenada - & I have relatives all over the Caribbean. I'm the only representative of that part of the world to drive in Formula 1, so when Top Gear told me about the event I said straight-away: "I'd love to do it". It was real y cool to go there and it was so busy. Thousands turned up. I heard folk flew in from Jamaica & Trinidad just to see me.

It was weird. It was almost like it was my event. In fact, Jeremy Clarkson said to the crowd at one point that "15% of the people are here to see Top Gear and 85% to see Lewis". It was unbelievable, really one of the best weekends I've ever had... the feeling, the energy I got. The fans were so excited - the most excited I 've ever seen them in my life. I don't think they've ever seen anything like that before, never heard an Formula One car anyway, so it was surreal to be the person to bring that to them & represent F1.

Cricket and football are the biggest sports in the Caribbean, but I've noticed that Formula 1 is increasing in popularity. The event was just a blast. I drove a Mercedes Formula One car & 'raced' against rally stunt driver Ken Block. We did 'doughnuts' and everything. I've been wanting to do something like that with Ken for a while & hope we'll be able to do something similar in the future.

While Barbados and a lot of other places in the Caribbean are beautiful, they're not wealthy. My auntie, for example, lives in Grenada in a shack that's no more than 15ft square. That's how my dad's dad lived before he came to England. I went to Barbados after visiting Haiti as part of my work as a Unicef ambassador. Every year, I'm trying to do more with charities. I've been working with Unicef for a couple of years now & I signed up with Save the Children during 2013. Haiti is a beautiful place in many respects, but poverty is a real problem. A lot of money was raised for Haiti after the terrible earthquake in 2010 and things got a bit better there for a while, but conditions have started to deteriorate again & the child mortality rate has begun to increase.

No-one should have to live in the conditions that I saw some kids in there. They were malnourished, not eating. We've all seen pictures of children with flies on their faces, sad and hungry, but TV simply doesn't do justice to the tragedy of it. When you see a 2-year-old kid who doesn't have the energy to move, it's devastating. It brings tears to my eyes thinking about it now. I want to bring as much attention to that sort of thing as I can & the film I made there will be shown as part of Sport Aid on 8th June.

It's Monaco this weekend, a race I always look forward to. I like street tracks and this is one of my favourites, although my feelings about it have changed over the years. My win there during 2008 was one of the most significant events of my career, but this is my 8th year in F1 now & I've come to realise that there are so many other great races. Now Monaco is my home, the race is still special but it's different. The first few times I came here, I wanted to emulate Ayrton Senna and win, drive through the tunnel & around all those iconic corners.

I lived the dream - and still am living the dream - but the rose-tinted spectacles I once had have gone. Maybe it's like a relationship... there's the honeymoon period then it settles down into normality. It's still great, but it moves to a different level. I'll still get a buzz every time I climb into the car this weekend & I still want to be on the top of that podium on Sunday, but more than anything, I hope it's a good battle. Those 1st couple of years that I was in Formula 1, Monaco was great, fighting with McLaren team-mate Fernando Alonso in 2007 then the Ferraris the following year.

Since then there's only been a proper battle between teams vying for victory in a very few races . Whoever has the superior car has won. For me that's taken the passion away a little bit. Competition is what I live for. That's why I never play mind games. Of course, sometimes you say things without realising the implications, but I want to win on the track through pure ability. It's the way I was raised. I certainly don't want to handicap a rival before a race. I want him to be at his best then when I beat him that's bigger than any psychological ploy'.

"I thought my heart was going to explode", said Lewis Hamilton of the moment when he thought that the World Championship was slipping from his grasp for the 2nd year running. In the McLaren garage, the team were making rapid calculations but the family, led by Lewis, were facing up to another setback as he began the last lap 13 secs behind Timo Glock. They were 13 secs which Hamilton Jnr. didn't believe he could make up, thinking that he had to overtake Sebastian Vettel, who'd slipped past a couple of laps earlier, but Lewis couldn't get close to his Toro Rosso rival.

"I was pushing to get close to Sebastian, who was very quick. It just got harder and harder & I heard that I had to get past him and I was pushing but I couldn't get close enough. I didn't know where Glock was & Vettel was the guy to beat. I couldn't catch him, so at that point I was going to finish 6th. My heart was in my mouth. I don't know how I kept my cool. I don't know what would've happened if I'd lost out on the last lap", said Hamilton. It was so close that Lewis didn't realise he was world champion for several secs after he crossed the line: "I was shouting 'Do I have it? Do I have it?'"

In the McLaren garage, the celebrations were led by Hamilton's family including his dad Anthony and Nicolas, his brother. Lewis has often stated that Nic is his main inspiration for the way he not only copes with cerebral palsy but remains so positive: "I often try to imagine myself in Nic's position. I don't think I'd be anywhere near as strong as him. There's just so much to admire in him, so whatever I'm doing, I say to myself 'If you think it's hard to do this then think again'". Victory was all the sweeter for coming in the home town of the late Ayrton Senna, Formula One legend & Hamilton's boyhood hero: "I'm very emotional, I've cried. My heart's feeling so much strain right now. I think first and foremost of my family then I thank God, because he was with me all year as he always is".

The championship was vindication for the support of Ron Dennis, the McLaren team boss, who was approached by the young Lewis when he was still a schoolboy: "It's a fairytale story that he gave me that opportunity years ago & he had the foresight to bring me in then groom me to get to this position. I've paid him back in full, so I'm happy with that", said Lewis. If he retained his crown, Ron would owe him a limited- edition £2 million McLaren F1 LM, top speed 225mph, which was promised if he won 2 championships. He had the front half.

"I had a lot of racism growing up where I grew up. I was bullied at school but it definitely encouraged me. It's like battle wounds - you come out the other side and it just makes you tougher. My dad always said, 'Do your talking on the track', so from day one I always did my talking on the track. 'Let your results speak louder than anything you have to say. You don't have to say anything to these people', but you know, I had kids shouting stuff, teachers that told me, 'You're never going to be a racing driver, you'll never amount to anything'. Just really trying to pull you down'", said Lewis Hamilton.

He added that the hostile reaction hadn't let up once he started competing in karting events around the country: "We arrived, the go-kart was stuffed in the back of the boot & all these folk had tents,

RVs, the best of stuff, but we were just so amateur. It wasn't like they stopped - but they all looked. All eyes were on us. 'What are they doing here?' We were the only black family and it was just like that every weekend when we arrived".

Hamilton said that he'd previously been warned not to speak out about racial issues to avoid upsetting sponsors and fans, but that he felt it was important to speak honestly about such important matters. "I've been in this sport for a long time now & it's kind of been like, 'Don't get into that subject, don't talk too much about it'. It's always been an issue and for sure folk in the limelight are guarded about what they've built and created. I see the things that go on & I feel a certain way about it, but it's about making sure if you're saying something, if you're doing something, it's for the right reasons in the right way. It's just hard to strike a balance, I think".

Lewis said that it was why he was able to shrug off criticism of his lifestyle. "There was a point when I actually cared and I guess just with age, I got to the point where I don't need your validation. I know my heart. I know how hard I work. I know my values. I know the love for my family. I know who I am as a person & I enjoy my life".

Lewis Hamilton set the world on fire with his very 1st serious run in a Formula 1 car. At Silverstone, during September 2006, a 21-year-old Hamilton was given an evaluation test by McLaren as the team considered his promotion to Formula One the following year. McLaren's race driver Pedro de la Rosa was there as a benchmark. The engineers preparing the car knew Lewis had talent - the team had been supporting his career for the previous 8 years - but like most other drivers they were expecting him to need time to adjust to the extreme demands of a Grand Prix car.

They were wrong, as after a couple of familiarisation runs, Hamilton was given a set of new tyres then was matching De la Rosa's times: "Just looking at the data for a couple of seconds, I realised we had a massive problem - me and all the other drivers on the grid. When I saw the strength of Lewis, I realised this guy is on a different level", Pedro recalled. The test team reported back to the factory that Hamilton was 'incredible', so before long his place in the team for 2007, as team-mate to double world champion Fernando Alonso, was confirmed. It was, said Martin Whitmarsh, McLaren's chief executive officer at the time "One of the easier decisions".

F1's greatest debut season followed, Lewis being unlucky not to win the title, but pushed on a year later, as one of the most dramatic finales in sporting history made him the youngest ever Formula 1 world champion. Year after year, Hamilton went on producing moments that were carved into Formula One legend. Jaw-dropping qualifying laps followed by remarkable race drives continued through his campaigns with McLaren then his later move to Mercedes, where he'd not only dominated on the track for the previous 7 years but become a global icon with a reach far beyond his sport. There'd also been a few controversies along the way.

Many of those who'd shared the journey with him thought that Lewis was fair, generous, respectful, honest & honourable, but also ruthless, focused, self-obsessed and ultra-competitive; insular & intense but also warm and open. He became the most successful driver in the history of F1, breaking Michael Schumacher's record of 91 wins, while equalling the German's record of 7 world championships in 2020.

Hamilton's route to unprecedented success started at Rye House, an unassuming wee go-kart track, tucked between a supermarket distribution centre and a nature reserve, at the junction of a couple of railway lines, just off the A10 in Hertfordshire. It was there that Lewis went when aged 8, with his father Anthony & a 2nd-hand kart, taking his 1st step on to the motor-sport ladder. He stood out straight away, not only because he was good but because he didn't look like any of the other kids he was racing.

Motor racing, like many sports requiring financial clout, attracting the better-off members of society, is notoriously lacking in diversity, Formula 1 never having had a black driver. Hamilton's paternal family were neither wealthy, nor white, his grandparents having come to the UK from the Caribbean Spice Island of Grenada during the '50s. Anthony grew up in west London then wed a white woman, Carmen, the couple having Lewis in January 1985, before splitting up when he was aged 2.

His dad lived in a council house in Stevenage, while working in IT for the railways and taking on extra jobs to support Lewis's racing, including selling double glazing, washing dishes & putting up 'for sale' boards for estate agents. "I had to buy a trailer to put the go-kart on and spare tyres, this, that & the other. The credit cards were all maxed out", Anthony recalled.

Money wasn't the only problem, as the Hamiltons were usually the only black folk at races, and there was racial abuse: "The first time it happened, I felt really upset & told my mum and dad. I felt like I needed to get revenge but lately, if anyone says anything to me, I just ignore them then get them back on the track", a young Lewis once stated.

Hamilton Jnr. became the youngest ever winner of the British cadet kart championship when 10 years old, during 1995. That year he attended the Autosport Awards, the motor-sport industry's end-of-season shindig, walking up to Ron Dennis, the boss of McLaren, introduced himself then said: "One day, I want to be racing your cars". 3 years later, after Lewis had won his 2nd British karting championship, Dennis signed him up to McLaren's driver development programme.

Martin Whitmarsh was put in charge of overseeing Hamilton's career: "He had this youthful, naive, warm personality about him. You wanted him to make it. I don't know whether I could've said back then that he was going to be a multiple world champion, you just saw that he was a really likeable kid who came from a modest background, had a pretty pushy father. He wasn't arrogant or cocky. There are a few things he's done in his life where from afar you think, 'Oh, God, Lewis...' but actually he's not bad. He's got a sincere humility about him. That lad came up & you thought, 'There's something here. It's got to be worth a punt'".

Before long, success started to come - but not, at times, fast enough for either Hamilton Jnr. or his dad. Lewis won the UK Formula Renault Championship in 2003 then after finishing 4th in the Formula 3 Euroseries the following year, he and Anthony wanted to move straight up to GP2, the final category before Formula 1. Martin disagreed, believing that Hamilton Jnr. would learn more by staying in F3 to dominate the championship during 2005:

"We had a huge row. I was accused of ruining his career by holding him back in F3. By that time Lewis was getting a bit of traction & his father felt there were other options. In the end, I took the contract out and tore it up. I freed them. I said, 'I don't want you here under duress. We want to work with you. This is what I really want you to do. If you don't want to do it...' It was c. 6 weeks before Lewis rang me then we re-signed. I look back now & think, 'I could've been the person who tore Lewis Hamilton's contract up and never got him back'. I was so lucky, really", Whitmarsh recalled.

Hamilton did what was asked of him, dominating European F3 in 2005 before moving up to GP2 the following year, driving one of the most impressive seasons the championship - which became known as Formula 2 - had ever seen. F1 beckoned. Fernando Alonso, who'd joined McLaren for 2007 after winning 2 successive titles with Renault, was unimpressed when told that his new team-mate would be a newbie.

Martin said: "Fernando was, 'Well, why are we doing that? If we're going to try to win the championship, we don't need a kid in the car, we need someone experienced. I need a strong team-mate; we don't need a rookie', but it turned out to be quite a different story". What followed was a dramatic, tumultuous season during which perhaps the strongest driver pairing ever put together in Formula One came close to tearing McLaren apart.

Lewis was on the podium for his 1st 9 races in a row, winning his 7th, with the Italian media labelling him 'Il Fenomeno' - the phenomenon but at McLaren, the tension was rising. As the man who'd ended Michael Schumacher's domination of Formula One with Ferrari, Alonso had established himself as the sport's leading driver. Although it wasn't in his contract, the Spaniard felt his status demanded that he was McLaren's team leader & designated championship contender but Hamilton had other ideas.

During the 1st race of the season, Fernando qualified in 2nd and Lewis 4th, but at the start Hamilton pulled a stroke that set the tone for what was to come. He overtook his team-mate around the outside of the first corner then ran confidently ahead of him for 2/3 of the race. Alonso finished 2nd behind Ferrari's Kimi Raikkonen in the end, with Hamilton 3rd, but the 'kid' had left a huge impression, which just kept growing. "He turned out to be the best rookie that there's ever been. Because actually, more remarkable almost than 7 championships & the most wins, his 1st half-season is just the most extraordinary in history", said Paddy Lowe, then McLaren's technical director.

Lewis first led the championship after the 4th race of the season, taking it away from Fernando at the Spaniard's home Grand Prix. The problems that led to the team unravelling began at the next race in Monaco, where Alonso dominated the race from pole, building a sizeable lead over Hamilton. After both drivers had made their final pit stops, Fernando backed off to cruise to the end. Both had been told to be wary of overheating rear brake calipers but Lewis closed up to his team-mate then started pressuring him.

With a 1-2 in the bag, and no prospect of Hamilton passing Alonso, the team ordered him to slow down but he refused then after the race revealed his dissatisfaction to the world. "It started to go wrong there. Lewis should've heeded the instructions of the team not to take excessive risk on that occasion, but in fairness to him, he hadn't had a win at that stage & he was hungry to have one. If he'd been the subservient instruction-obeyer, he wouldn't be the Lewis Hamilton who's won 7 world championships, would he?" Martin said.

Hamilton's maiden victory followed soon after, in dominant fashion, at the very next race in Canada. Through that long, tense summer, the advantage swung back and forth between him & Fernando, with Raikkonen and his Ferrari team-mate Felipe Massa also in the mix for the championship. Ramping up the pressure, the title battle took place against the political backdrop of the 'spy-gate' case, in which McLaren's chief designer had been found with of 780 pgs. of confidential Ferrari technical information.

The next flashpoint was the Hungarian Grand Prix, where what was meant to happen was for Alonso to run first on track ahead of Lewis during qualifying. McLaren had been alternating which of their drivers would benefit from a complex 2007 rule relating to fuel loads, it being Fernando's turn but Hamilton went out ahead instead, refusing repeated requests over the radio to let Alonso through. This disadvantaged Fernando in the fight for pole, who'd worked out what was going on, making sure that he came into the pits 1st, before their final laps.

As Alonso's new tyres were being fitted, Lewis was waiting behind for his. With the work rapidly completed, Fernando then held his car, having calculated how long he'd need to block Hamilton to make sure he wouldn't be able to start his final lap, only pulling away when he was sure that Lewis was out of time. All hell broke loose, Ron throwing his headphones down in disgust before going over to remonstrate with Alonso's trainer, who he wrongly believed was involved. The drivers were called to the stewards, who were also visited by Anthony Hamilton, Fernando being given a 5-place grid penalty.

The next morning, still furious, Alonso met Dennis, threatening to go to the FIA with information relating to the spy-gate case unless the team put Lewis at a disadvantage in the race. Fernando later withdrew the threat, but it was too late, his relationship with McLaren having been irrevocably broken. A contract that had been meant to run for 3 years was terminated by mutual consent at the end of the year.

"Lewis didn't co-operate with the team or Fernando & that was straightforward disobeying. He impetuously wanted to win. When thinking about signing a driver, having a daughter as I do, I'd think,

'Would I be happy for my daughter to bring him home?' If the answer was 'Yes', you'd say, 'OK, I don't think I want to sign him'. You wanted a driver who if your daughter brought them home, you'd think, 'Oh, God, she's going to get hurt', because they're so selfish and self-possessed. As much as I love Lewis to death, would I be happy for my daughter to bring him home? No. As part of the complex equation of talent, intensity, focus, they also have to have a bit of ruthlessness. Lewis had that & he was bloody young. Would he be any different today? Probably not, and that was it, just bloody minded", said Whitmarsh.

Hamilton won that race, but finished off the podium in both Turkey & Belgium, either side of a runners-up place behind Alonso in Italy. A brilliant win in Japan followed, in torrential rain that led Fernando to crash then Lewis went to the penultimate race in China with a chance of clinching the title in his debut season. Instead, McLaren "Just got it wrong", in Martin's words. Hamilton led from pole on a drying track, but the team left him out for too long on worn tyres. When he was called into the pits, tyres down to the canvas, he slid off the track in the pit lane, getting beached in a gravel trap. Kimi Raikkonen won from Alonso, which left Lewis leading the championship by 4 points from Fernando and 7 from Kimi going into the decider in Brazil, during October 2007.

It should've been enough, but Hamilton's hopes evaporated. After qualifying 2nd behind Felipe Massa, his 1st lap was messy. He lost places to Raikkonen & Alonso in the first couple of corners then ran off the track trying to pass Fernando around the outside of turn 4, dropping to 8th. Lewis was up to 6th within 4 laps, but then his car had a problem with an hydraulic valve, which was blocked for 25 secs, during which time the car was stuck in 4th gear. The blockage flushed through but by then Hamilton had dropped down to 18th place.

Massa dominated the race but Ferrari held him at his final pit stop long enough to gift Kimi the win. It was just enough for the Finn to take the title, with Lewis and Alonso 1 point behind. If Felipe had won, as he would've without team intervention, Hamilton would've been champion on results count back. With Raikkonen victorious, Lewis needed 5th place, but finished a couple of positions short. Looking back, Hamilton said: "I remember the build-up to those races at the end & the pressure was there. That wasn't needed. If I knew then what I know now, I would've easily won that championship. I think that I've learnt not to add unnecessary pressure". The disappointment of losing was softened by the knowledge that nobody had ever performed better in a debut season and everyone knew that there was much more to come.

A year later, Lewis was back in Brazil, with another championship on the line, Sao Paulo native Massa being his closest rival. Memories of the previous championship slipping through their fingers were still painfully fresh at McLaren, when at a public appearance the night before the race, someone threw a toy black cat on to the stage in front of Hamilton. "It really spooked Lewis. I remember going up to see him in his room on the Saturday night. Closing out the championship, after what had happened the year before... That was a time when I felt we needed to be a little bit gentle and supportive. Most of the time, you didn't need to - Lewis knew what he was capable of & quietly had that self-belief", Whitmarsh recalled.

It was an agonising weekend, with McLaren, knowing Hamilton needed only to finish 5th to clinch the title even if Felipe won, taking an overly conservative approach, as Paddy Lowe stated, which led to one of the most spectacular finishes the sport has ever seen. Lewis qualified 4th then in damp conditions kept that position at the start as Massa led through 2 sets of pit stops on a drying track. Late in the race, there was more rain, so most of the drivers stopped for wet-weather tyres, but Toyota's Timo Glock didn't, which allowed the German to move up the field, with Hamilton dropping to 5th.

The rain came down more heavily with a couple of laps to go, as Lewis ran wide, letting Sebastian Vettel's Toro Rosso slip ahead into 5th place, so the title was in Felipe's hands. Hamilton fought to re-pass Sebastian but couldn't, so as they raced around the final lap, it seemed like it was all over. Massa was about to win and Lewis, a place behind where he needed, was on the verge of missing out for the 2nd consecutive year. "I don't know what Lewis was feeling in the car, but we just couldn't believe we were having a repeat of the previous year. It was like, 'God, what do we have to do around here to win a championship?'" remembered Paddy.

As Felipe crossed the line, Hamilton was still in 6th, so in the Ferrari pit, they began to celebrate what they thought was the world championship title, but out on track Glock was struggling in the wet on his worn slick tyres & Lewis was catching him up. He passed the Toyota as it slithered out of the final corner, to take the 5th place that he needed to clinch his 1st title. As the celebrations suddenly came to an end in the Ferrari pit, at McLaren they went wild, with Hamilton's family - dad Anthony, half-brother Nicolas and Pussy Cat Girl friend Nicole Scherzinger - joining them. "That was quite a moment for me, him & everybody in the team. For a couple of minutes I was going to give up Formula 1", Lowe said.

Lewis had made history, at the end of an up-and-down year that had a number of stand-out moments, one in particular remaining one of his finest victories. The British Grand Prix of 2008 was wet but Hamilton was out of this world, in a league way beyond anyone else on track that day. As conditions ebbed & flowed, at times Lewis was lapping 5 secs quicker than any other driver, winning by 1 min. 8 secs, while Massa spun 5 times. Only a couple of other drivers finished on the same lap, Lewis' team-mate, Heikki Kovalainen, who finished 5th, not being one of them.

It was a performance comparable with some of the greatest wet-weather drives in history - Jackie Stewart winning by 4 mins at the Nurburgring in 1968; Ayrton Senna's 1st victory in Portugal during 1985; Schumacher's first win for Ferrari in Spain in 1996. Hamilton produced many similar performances over the years, where he was on another level beyond his rivals, so how did he do it? Driving an F1 car involves skills that most ordinary folk find difficult to understand. After braking at the very last possible point, the driver is balancing on the edge of grip during cornering, an exercise that could be likened to walking a tightrope at 100mph down a steep hill around a corner in high wind. It's a pursuit that, in the words of Mercedes technical director James Allison, requires "sublime delicacy and unbelievable levels of concentration and precision".

As McLaren's test driver from 2007-9, Pedro De la Rosa observed Hamilton's talents more closely than most. Having worked with both, he rated Lewis & Fernando as the 2 best drivers that he'd ever seen first hand, including Michael Schumacher. Where they differentiated themselves from the rest, he said, was in the entry phase of a corner: "Where they are special, Lewis and Fernando, is how much speed they can run into the apex & still have a decent exit speed. It's very easy to say; it's very difficult to do. Most drivers, over 1 lap, when the rear tyres are at their peak grip, can do that, so if you look at Valtteri Bottas, for example, over 1 lap many times he's matching Lewis. The problem comes when the rear tyres drop off. That's when they are so much better than the rest. They still keep the speed going in".

Paddy Lowe said that an ability to control his car in this way not only "makes you go faster in the moment, but also allows you to set the car up to be nearer the limit, so it's inherently quicker". Those skills also explained why Hamilton was often so much more effective in races than Bottas, when it came to key techniques, including following another car closely, overtaking or keeping tyres in optimum condition.

"Some drivers can't get that close to the car in front, but Lewis and Fernando always can, when they're behind they're nearly touching the gearbox. You can see that they're following in a different manner, in an aggressive manner, in a way that isn't comfortable at all for the car in front. You lose a lot of grip when you're following - especially with these modern F1 cars - but that type of driver knows how to compensate by balancing with speed & brakes. It doesn't really matter if the car is under-steering or over-steering, they'll sort the balance out with their feeling. They don't know why they're doing it. They just know it's faster and that's all talent - pure, raw talent".

However, ability wasn't all it took to win in Formula One. If an inferior driver had an inherently superior car, there was little even someone as good as Hamilton could do about it. Over the final 4 seasons of Lewis' time at McLaren, from 2009 to 2012, the machinery didn't always match his standards, so Red Bull had 4 years of domination with Vettel, while he was growing up in the public eye, with personal problems adversely affecting his professional life.

Hamilton Jnr. told his dad that he no longer wanted him to be his manager during 2010, the pair not speaking for a while. "It was the worst time of my life. It's difficult to explain it. I think I probably was too much of an ogre. It was, 'Lewis, do this, do that', and it was, 'Come on, Dad, I'm a grown man'. That's probably when he rebelled. He didn't do it when he was 15, he did it when he was a world champion & it was all my fault, because as a parent I forgot how to let go. Lewis said, 'Do you know what, Dad? I have to go and do my own thing'", Anthony said.

Lewis split with Nicole Scherzinger in early 2011. "He was very upset about that. He did love Nicole", said Matt Bishop, McLaren's former communications director. Hamilton was destabilised, making an uncharacteristic series of mistakes that year, many of them crashes with Felipe Massa. Perhaps no incident better summed up Lewis' anguished state of mind than what happened in Monaco, where he finished 6th after getting 2 penalties during the race: "It's an absolute frickin' joke. I've been to see the stewards 5 times out of 6 this season", he said afterwards.

Asked why that was the case, Hamilton replied: "Maybe it's because I'm black. That's what Ali G says", the remark causing a storm. Chief steward Lars Osterlind & FIA president Jean Todt took offence at the implication that Lewis' skin colour had influenced the decisions, there being a chance that he could've been banned from a number of races. However, McLaren officials persuaded Hamilton to issue the statement that he "never meant to offend anyone", so the matter was dropped.

Looking back through the prism of what Lewis has become, the racial abuse that he suffered early in his career, and the anti-racism stance that he's since adopted, the incident can be seen in a different light. It's clear that being Formula 1's only black competitor has never been far from the front of Hamilton's mind. His Mercedes team boss Toto Wolff related: "He asked me once, 'Have you ever had the active thought that you're white?' I replied, 'I've never thought about it'. He said, 'I think about it every day'.

That was a year or 2 ago & it triggered a profound reflection within me, because we as a majority white people in European countries, never think about it. Imagine you enter the paddock and you're the only white person & how difficult that'd be. I guess it'd make you think about your skin colour every day then if you add abuse & racism to the whole equation, it becomes unbearable. This is what he and many others around the world are facing every day".

Martin Whitmarsh, who's been appointed as one of the members of the commission Lewis has set up to look into the lack of diversity in the UK motor-sport industry, pointed out that a very similar incident to Monaco 2011 almost happened at the Russian Grand Prix of 2020, when Hamilton accused F1 bosses of "trying to stop me" after he was given a penalty for 2 illegal practice starts. "One of the learnings I'm having right now, is that I've gone through life not taking racism seriously enough. Because it hasn't affected me; I haven't witnessed it at close hand, so I therefore do think that if you've experienced racism in your life at any point - & sadly if you're black or not white in a predominantly white society, you've probably experienced it more than folk realise - it must then subconsciously be in your mind as to why people appear to not be giving you the rub in critical situations.

Lewis is super-competitive and super-ruthless. It really deeply hurts him if he doesn't win the race on Sunday afternoon, so he's going to look for reasons - within himself, the team, the tyres, the officials, whatever. He's going to be looking for that reason, because he has that passion, that strong desire, that will & that need to win", Martin stated. In the end, the lack of a 2nd championship at McLaren got to Hamilton, so he started looking for a move away. He was courted by Mercedes from early 2012, then led by team boss Ross Brawn and commercial director Nick Fry. McLaren had a faster car, with Mercedes having struggled during the 3 years since they'd taken over the title-winning Brawn team at the end of 2009, so few expected Lewis to make the jump, but jump he did.

Lewis spoke of needing a change, a fresh challenge & his belief in Mercedes' chance of success in the future, all of which was true, but there was more to the decision. Late that summer, Hamilton had a big row with Ron Dennis, who'd made some damaging personal accusations about his driver to Daimler boss Dieter Zetsche, in a vain attempt to stop Mercedes signing him. When Ron's actions got back to Lewis via intermediaries, he was furious, his relationship with Dennis being over in his mind. It stayed that way for a long while before they extended olive branches to each other Hamilton, aged 27, felt loyalty to McLaren, but wanted to get away.

Nick Fry told of an exhausting few days as negotiations over the details of the Mercedes contract reached their critical point over the weekend of the Singapore Grand Prix, during September 2012. At 1st Mercedes were £3-4m short of the £30m fee Lewis and his manager Simon Fuller were demanding, so they had to lean on title sponsor Petronas for more money. There were negotiations over the use of Hamilton's image rights.

He led the race in his McLaren until his gearbox failed, giving victory to Sebastian Vettel. He had a final meeting with Mercedes non-executive chairman Niki Lauda in his hotel room then by the end of that weekend, a deal had been put together on which all parties had agreed. Lewis flew to Thailand for a holiday before the next race in Japan, where the contract was sent over to him from Mercedes via his lawyer, Sue Thackeray.

After a few days he called Martin Whitmarsh to tell him that he was leaving McLaren. "That was one of the most difficult moments. I've been a very loyal person, I'd been with McLaren since I was 13, so to decide to leave a team that had given me a place in the sport then to call your boss to tell them you're leaving was damaging & emotionally difficult", said Hamilton.

"He was very cosseted at McLaren, very controlled by 2 individuals he wanted to divorce himself from, his dad and Dennis. They'd contributed to his growth but ultimately limited it. I think he had the belief that he had to become his own man & he had to be able to survive and grow further without those 2 dominant characters. It was the most difficult decision of his life. He was emotional about it, but at the time, I sensed that it was the right decision for him & subsequently it's proven to be just that", Martin stated.

On a grey, humid Saturday afternoon at Japan's Suzuka circuit, Lewis' championship hopes of 2016 were unravelling before the world's eyes. A couple of hours before, his Mercedes team-mate Nico Rosberg had beaten him to pole position by 0.013 secs. The Formula 1 media filed into Mercedes' base in the paddock to hear Hamilton's thoughts. They'd hear them, but not in the way that they expected, as he made a short speech, in which he talked about a lack of respect, revealed his lack of enthusiasm for any questions then walked out.

Lewis' move to Mercedes had paid off better and earlier than he'd ever expected. After a building year in 2013, the introduction of F1's hybrid engine regulations brought success, with a car miles ahead of the rest of the field, so Hamilton won the championships of 2014 & 2015. He did it the hard way during 2014, three times overhauling a points advantage built up by Nico while Hamilton suffered problems. Lewis won his 3rd title at a canter the following year, dominating from the start to clinch the championship with 3 races to go.

However, 2016 turned into a rerun of 2014 - only worse, a bad start at the opening race of the season followed by engine failures in qualifying at 2 of the next 3 Grands Prix put Hamilton on the back foot, 43 pts behind Rosberg after just 4 races. Just as a couple of years earlier, Lewis clawed it back, despite hiccups along the way. He had a bad start here and there, an off weekend in Azerbaijan, but by late summer he was leading the drivers' championship, only for a grid penalty at the Belgian Grand Prix, a legacy of earlier engine failures, to knock him back again. There was another difficult weekend for Hamilton in Singapore, where he never seemed to get it together, allowing Nico back in front.

As Lewis led the next race in Malaysia, with Singapore was behind him, winning would give him a comfortable lead, one he thought he could hold on to for the rest of the season. However, his engine went bang again. "Oh no!" he screamed over the team radio, before kneeling down beside the smoking car, helmet in hands. Hamilton could hardly believe it. Why was it happening to him? Not long after getting out of the car, he said to the TV cameras: "Something or someone doesn't want me to win this year". Was Lewis alluding to a conspiracy theory within Mercedes to allow Rosberg to win? An hour or so later, he clarified: "A higher power. It feels right now as if the man above or a higher power is intervening a little bit".

Hamilton went on Instagram couple of days later with a series of posts praising the team. After arriving at Suzuka, he seemed a distracted figure at the official news conference before the Japanese Grand Prix, refusing to answer questions, repeatedly referring journalists back to his social media posts, while spending his time putting pictures of himself and fellow drivers on Snapchat using the animal-face filter. The British newspapers weren't impressed, producing a series of pieces criticising Lewis' behaviour. 'Snap prat' being the Sun's headline.

Shortly after the news conference, Nico bumped into a journalist, who told him what had gone on. "Did he?" asked the German. "Good", Rosberg sensing an opportunity. The maths of the championship race were clear - if he could win in Japan, he would have enough of a lead to finish 2nd behind Hamilton at all the remaining races but still win the title, which given the magnitude of Mercedes' advantage over the field, should've been relatively easy, reliability permitting. Nico was quickest throughout the weekend, just holding off Hamilton for pole.

At Lewis' post-session news conference he said "I'm not here to answer your questions, I've decided. The other day was a super light-hearted thing & if I was disrespectful to any of you guys, or if you felt I was disrespectful, it was honestly not the intention. It was just a little bit of fun, but what was more disrespectful was what was then written worldwide. I don't really plan on sitting here many more times for these kind of things, so my apologies, but I hope you guys enjoy the rest of your weekend".

The following day, Hamilton fussed over a damp patch on the track near his grid slot before the race then made a bad start, finishing only 3rd behind Rosberg and Red Bull's Max Verstappen. Rosberg's lead had increased to 33 pts with just 4 races left. All Lewis could do was win them all, while hoping that some misfortune befell Nico in one of them. Hamilton did win them - but it wasn't enough. At the final race in Abu Dhabi, Lewis made it difficult for his team-mate, putting him under pressure by backing him towards Vettel's Ferrari, but Rosberg held on to seal the championship.

"I saw Nico when he got back to the garage & we were sort of out of sight. He just hugged me, burst into tears then said, 'That was so terrible. It was so difficult'. It was Lewis' mastery of the situation, without being unsporting", Paddy Lowe said. After the race in Abu Dhabi, Hamilton pointed out that he'd lost the championship because of the skewed reliability record between the pair, but in the garage Paddy, who'd moved to Mercedes at the same time as Lewis, sensed that his defeat would prove to be bad news for the rest of the grid:

"What he's learned, become better at, and now unbeatable because of, is to be always present at 110%. I'm sure it's a 10-year process, but 2016 was a very significant turning point. I remember at the time thinking, 'Well, that's just never going to happen again. Lewis is now unbeatable, because he's gonna turn up at maximum performance for every event'", said Lowe.

That season finished Rosberg off. It had taken so much effort, focus & commitment to beat Hamilton to the championship title, even with all the luck that had gone his way, using every trick he knew, on-track and off, psychological games & more, that he decided he couldn't face going through it all again. His lifetime ambition achieved, he quit at the end of the season. Nico was sure he wouldn't beat Hamilton again, but who could?

When Lewis came back in 2017, with a new team-mate in Bottas, he never again brought up the engine failures and reliability issues when he was discussing the previous season, only his own errors. A lesson had been learned, never to be forgotten, his driving having since risen to a new level. The speed remained, wedded to a new solidity & consistency, becoming almost unstoppable, even when he hadn't got the best equipment.

Hamilton had identified his weaknesses, the bad starts and off weekends of 2016. the relative struggles in qualifying of 2019 then worked on them, while retaining the strengths that he'd always had, so it'd become tough to find any flaws. Toto Wolff said "His ability to question himself & to develop is really amazing. It's not something you see very often in champions. I guess with many others who become world champion or win a great title there are several risks - a sense of entitlement, a certain complacency which kicks in, which is perfectly understandable. The great champions don't stop pushing themselves further and further & further. That's what I see from Lewis Hamilton the driver and from Lewis Hamilton the person".

The driving force behind what Toto called his "relentless push for perfection" was Lewis' intense dislike of losing. His former team-mate Pedro De la Rosa saw it up close: "Every winter we went to Finland for a week's training camp. He was so competitive, man. It's unbelievable. No matter what sport we played, Lewis always had to win & he was so good at everything. He's just naturally talented at almost any sport. If we were climbing, he was the best in the team. Whatever we did, it was, 'Man, Lewis is winning again'. It was a bit embarrassing. The only sport I beat him at was tennis, and only in one game, because he realised that he had no chance against me, so he never, ever wanted to play against me again".

Mercedes chief engineer Andrew Shovlin added: "You can't ask Lewis to be happy when he's lost a race; that's not how he works, but he loses really well if you want someone to come back to win the next one. He's actually better at losing than most I've seen, because of how diligently he goes through the block of work of understanding what he needs to be better, where did he miss the opportunities.

He doesn't enjoy it, but it's about the result at the next race, not whether he's smiling or giving a nice interview. Lewis has natural talent in abundance, but his work ethic & ability to continually develop and improve means that, for drivers trying to beat him, he's a bit of a moving target. The thing with Lewis now is his bad days are so few & far between and even on his bad days he's as good as the others. That's what's brought him to the level he's at. It's the consistency, and when he's at his best, the level is just phenomenal".

James Allison who'd worked alongside Michael Schumacher, Fernando Alonso, Sebastian Vettel & Hamilton during his 30-year career said: "Useless parlour game though it is, I personally think Lewis is the finest of them. As a racing car driver, I think he's the fastest and most likely to win any championship between the world champions I've been lucky enough to work with, but it's not just that. The thing I find remarkable about him is that he's as much of a carnivore as the rest of them in his dogged need to win, but he's got a line & it's a line all the rest of us would want to admire in the way he handles himself as a sportsman and the way he interacts with us as a man. That's what sets him apart in my mind & why I think I'll always have a soft spot for him".

The combination of the greatest Formula One team ever assembled with one of the fastest and best drivers of all time, both of whom shared an unquenchable desire to push on to the next level, had led to unprecedented levels of success at Mercedes & the more Hamilton got, the more he'd had his eyes opened to what he could do with it. Over the years, Lewis had become increasingly vocal on causes that mattered to him. It started with environmentalism, followed by going vegan, because of his concerns for the state of the planet then as the murder of George Floyd by US police sparked global fury in the summer of 2020, Hamilton spoke out on the horrors and injustices of racism.

It hadn't been easy going. He'd been central in Formula 1's decision to promote a pro-diversity agenda, but the messaging had left something to be desired. The fact that 7 F1 drivers chose not to take the knee alongside Lewis at the regular pre-race demonstrations had contrasted with the more united message coming from athletes in sports including football and basketball. However, his determination to speak out hadn't been affected, Hamilton not being shy of pushing the message to a point where some felt uncomfortable, or feathers were ruffled, as over his decision to wear a T-shirt highlighting another case of police brutality, the killing of Breonna Taylor, on the podium at the Tuscan Grand Prix of September 2020.

However, Lewis had won plaudits around the world for his stance on such issues. Along with his naming as one of Time magazine's 100 most influential people of that year was a tribute from Nascar driver Bubba Wallace, the only black competitor in a form of motor-sport with perhaps an even more serious diversity problem than F1. Wallace wrote that Hamilton's "activism has moved the world. Lewis's mental preparation, his aura, his ability to capitalise on every opportunity to use his platform to drive out racism are more than just a model for race-car drivers & other athletes - he's an inspiration for everyone".

Toto Wolff said: "He's almost philosophical about certain things. He spends a lot of time thinking. He's someone who hasn't built his whole life on one particular pillar. It all circles around his driving. He's the Formula One world champion, but now he's the Formula 1 world champion and he's a fighter for diversity, a fighter against racism. These are topics that go far beyond the racing driver. The topic of racism was always there & we discussed it. Every single year we discussed how we could increase the diversity within the team and he flagged that to me also - look at how many black folk are in the team, it's a super-minority & it's something none of us are really proud of.

Starting with Colin Kaepernick and then the terrible killing of George Floyd, Black Lives Matter & the global movement to fight against racism, for somebody like Lewis Hamilton, with the visibility and recognition he gets from outside, he felt it was important to use his voice. Just trying to fight against racism in your closed environment wasn't enough any more. It was about raising your voice & changing the tonality as well, to make himself heard, to make racism a topic nobody could ignore any more, even if it polarises or it's controversial. It's just the right thing to do".

Hamilton's unwillingness to simply be an F1 driver rubbed some folk up the wrong way, and he received criticism from some quarters for various reasons - he was too outspoken, he's contrived, he's too opinionated, too much of a poseur... but those who'd been close to him along the way painted a very different picture, including former McLaren team-mate De la Rosa :

"We spent a lot of time together, travelling. I remember being in Malaysia testing after the race in 2007. We were having dinner when suddenly a British newly married couple were sitting next to us, having recognised Lewis. Back then, he wasn't really well known. They wanted to take a picture but he said: 'Do you know me, or do you know Pedro?' then they said, 'No, no, we know you. We don't know Pedro'. He was a bit surprised. He was so modest. He invited them to our table. We were having a coffee together & I'm pretty sure for that married couple it was the best present for their honeymoon.

That was Lewis when he 1st came into Formula One. He was truly refreshing. He was really nice. I'm not in contact with him on a regular basis now, because I'm not attending the races, but when I see him, I feel that it's the same Lewis, and he's still that sweet boy I met when I was at McLaren when he was a kid. From the guy who was having dinner in Malaysia, he's changed. He wouldn't do that now, but he's had to change & that's what folk have to understand. Lewis is one of the icons of sport worldwide, and that's something we all have to accept, but his heart is in the right place & his heart doesn't forget, and that's really nice".

Hamilton's dad Anthony said he still couldn't quite believe what the boy from the council house in Stevenage had become: "I sit in admiration & awe of Lewis for everything that he's done. It's a fantastic thing. I'm thinking, 'Wow! You're not just a racing driver. You've become a statesman, a spokesman, a champion of causes for other folk'. You shouldn't be frightened to speak your mind. What you see with Lewis is a young man, a son, who has a heart, who has feelings, who cares for other people.

When I see folk criticise him for whatever lifestyle he may have led, well they don't really know him. What they see is his public persona. They see that he has money, gold chains and other bits & pieces, but that's nothing. What you see on the outside isn't what people are; it's what's on the inside and what's on the inside is a young man who had a dream when he was 8 years of age, worked hard, worked diligently, became the best in his field, honestly; is very kind, a very good son, a very good brother & is enjoying life".

Hamilton was 36 during January '21, his contract with Mercedes running out at the end of that year, but although he said after the Emilia Romagna Grand Prix that there was 'no guarantee' that he'd remain in Formula 1, on the same day he also stated that he wanted to 'continue to make history together' with Mercedes. A new contract seemed inevitable, as Lewis started 2021 as hot favourite to win an 8th world title, moving ahead in the record books.

"He's most aware that he's of a certain age, where you can see the effects on performance, but the way he's living his life, the way he looks after himself, being a vegan, the training that's constantly adapting to his age, the people he surrounds himself with, all that makes it possible for him to stretch his ability for top performance beyond an age where you'd normally think about ending your career. I think he has many more years in him to perform at the top level", said Wolff.

James added: "I hope his future is with us and glorious for a little while longer, because it works for us & I know he enjoys being part of this, but he's a person who's interesting and interested in lots of different things & is sufficiently driven that I imagine he'll pop up somewhere else doing something interesting. When he stops racing I very much doubt that it'll be the last the world hears of him".

At Silverstone, on 11th June 2006, with England in the grip of World Cup fever, the crowd for the British Grand Prix was expected to be down on recent years. There was little chance of any home success in the main event, but the stands and spectator banks were starting to fill up slowly as the GP2 race started at 9am. Lewis Hamilton had started down in 8th place, but was working his way through the field, with characteristic aggressive driving. He was soon closing in on the fight for 2nd place. Brazil's Nelson Piquet Junior & the Monegasque driver Clivio Piccione went through Copse side by side at c. 140mph, but as they accelerated out of the corner they were suddenly 3 wide as Lewis drew alongside.

Into the 5 sweeping bends that made up the daunting Becketts complex they went, with Piquet on the inside. Hamilton carried a lot of momentum around the outside of the 1st left-hander to claim the racing line and 2nd place as the road bore right then left again; Nelson drove straight through a temporary advertising hoarding. The cheers from the crowd were by far the loudest of the weekend as the young driver, then known only to hardcore petrol-heads, picked off the leader then cruised to victory. He was no longer unknown, as 'Lewis Hamilton + Silverstone' became one of the most popular searches on YouTube.

Had Britain's latest sporting hero-in-waiting heard the excitement of the crowd? Lewis said afterwards: 'I didn't, no. It all went silent at that point, because we were so close & I don't know if my body was preparing for something. You know when, if you're going to crash, your body gets ready to protect itself? I felt my body and the adrenaline all building up ready for something & when I came out it all relaxed, kind of saying, "Phew, thank God for that! I'm working my arse off, not only to do the best job possible, but also to get that seat at McLaren. I really want that. It's an opportunity not many folk get. If I can get that seat then I think - and I feel very confident - that I can make best use of it'.

A little under a year later, Hamilton not only had that seat at McLaren but after his 2nd place at the Spanish Grand Prix in Barcelona, was leading the Formula 1 drivers' championship. However, he was then back doing the unseen graft of testing. Along with the other 10 teams that were contesting the world championship, McLaren had moved on from Barcelona to the Paul Ricard circuit near Marseille in the south of France. The former home of the French Grand Prix had become a test track, albeit about the most sophisticated in the world - as one would expect from a facility owned by Bernie Ecclestone, the billionaire F1 ringmaster. Everything was of the highest standard & just as the proprietor would've liked, the team vehicles were lined up so precisely that they'd have done justice to the contents of David Beckham's fridge.

At the back of a grey McLaren bus, sheltered from the warm Mistral wind, sat Lewis Hamilton. It was 12 hrs since testing had begun, during which he'd driven 98 laps, posted the fastest time by over a second and been through a 2 1/2-hr debrief with his engineers. For a short while he was alone, staring at a computer screen with a diagram of the circuit & data on it. Not all his work was at 190mph in front of 140,000 folk.

After the excitement of a Grand Prix, testing must've seemed like a chore. Did it make him a better racer? 'I don't think so. You get that crafting from karting, the wheel-to-wheel racing you have there. The more racing you do the more you learn. I'm a racer naturally, so that's why I believe I'm good in the races. In the race it's all about consistency, and to get consistency you need to learn about the car & that comes from testing, but the test is mainly to build your awareness of what's around you, that you're understanding the car and to fine tune the car & yourself. Sometimes I don't make any changes to the car and I find half a second in myself. Some people find it really difficult, like the engineers, they say, "What can we do?" I say, "Don't do anything. I quite like the car as it is, I just need to improve myself"', stated Lewis.

He was trying to improve skills that had led to him making a record-breaking start to his Formula One career. He finished 3rd in his 1st race, the Australian Grand Prix then runner-up in Malaysia & Bahrain - a record run on the podium for a rookie, which he'd extended in Spain to become the youngest driver to lead the world championship. At the previous Sunday's Monaco Grand Prix, Hamilton finished 2nd once again, behind his McLaren team-mate, double world champion Fernando Alonso, but there were signs of frustration from the young Englishman at a victory missed, as he slipped to 2nd in the title race.

Lewis was called in for his 1st pit stop earlier than he expected, just as he was preparing to put in some really quick laps to extend his advantage over Alonso, who'd already stopped: 'I was actually quite surprised because I was fuelled to do 5 laps, maybe 6 laps, longer than Fernando but they stopped me with 3 laps to go. There wasn't much time to pull out a gap or improve my time; I wasn't really given much time for it. I came in 2 or 3 laps after him [Alonso]. That was unfortunate, but that's the way it goes. I've got # 2 on my car, I'm the # 2 driver, it's something I have to live with', Lewis said after the race.

McLaren's team principal, Ron Dennis, refuted allegations of team orders and race manipulation, which had been strictly against Formula 1 rules since 2002 when Ferrari instructed Rubens Barrichello to allow Michael Schumacher past to win the Austrian Grand Prix: 'We're scrupulously fair at all times in how we run this grand prix team. We'll never favour one driver, no matter who it is. We don't have team orders, we had a strategy to win this race. There'll be places where they'll be absolutely free to race, but this isn't one of them'. That last line had attracted the attention of the FIA, the sport's governing body, which started investigating 'incidents' concerning the McLaren team during the race.

Since his debut in Melbourne on 18th March '07, Hamilton had transformed the popularity of grand prix racing, not least because he was young, British, good looking & thrillingly fast. He was also mixed race in a sport that was overwhelmingly white; inevitably he'd been compared with Tiger Woods. 'I've never seen a rookie as good as him. Nobody has. He's coped with everything he's faced. He's been superb', said Damon Hill.

Triple world champion Sir Jackie Stewart was equally impressed. 'I think Lewis is going to rewrite the book. We'll see a new generation of what I call properly prepared, professional racing drivers. I'm talking about fully rounded; Michael Schumacher became that, but even Michael wasn't as good as he should've been, not in terms of the driving but the total package. I believe Lewis will create the benchmark for a whole generation of drivers. Niki Lauda and James Hunt changed the culture of racing drivers, but they weren't role models. They said nothing, didn't give a damn. Lewis Hamilton can become a role model'.

Even the unflappable Bernie Ecclestone was excited by Hamilton: 'He's got a lot of talent. The guy's a winner. It became clear pretty quickly that he'll win a grand prix some time - sooner rather than later.

He'll win the championship - but I don't think this year. It'd be asking a bit much & be a lot of pressure to expect that. It'd be fantastic if he did, but I don't think we should talk about that at this stage'.

When meeting Lewis it was hard not to be impressed or struck by just how young and fresh-faced he was, even when dressed up in McLaren T-shirt & jacket. He was courteous, intelligent, engaged and rarely lost eye contact, even if one sensed that he'd rather be getting on with some hardcore data analysis. Hamilton spoke enthusiastically of his time on the practice circuit. 'It's quite satisfying when you go out & you know that you needed to brake 10m later ... building up the courage to brake those 10m later, not lock up the tyres, and really pull it off. Sometimes you go into a corner thinking, "I'm not going to make it", but you say, "OK, we're going to do it" then you do it & you think, "Shoot, what was the big fuss in the 1st place", but you think about the advantage you've gained when you exit the corner - you're like, "Yeah, that was good". It's an amazing feeling'.

A Grand-Prix team can take more than 100 members to a race, not including the test team who work away from the public gaze. Lewis was keen to acknowledge that there were others who contributed to his success. 'Sometimes you don't even notice the changes the engineer has made. My engineer is so smart, he understands what I say and the way I communicate - that's a great feeling. When someone understands what you're talking about & is able to translate that into your car, it runs better'.

Hamilton had been supported by McLaren since Ron Dennis recruited him into the team's driver development programme as a 13-year-old in 1998. The team invested £5m in his career, offering technical support and advice as he worked his way up to the junior formulas. He graduated to racing cars during 2001, having won the championship in every series that he'd driven. The step up to Formula 1 was a natural progression & everything was done - including keeping him distant from the media - to ensure that Lewis was as prepared as possible. He'd appeared at the obligatory press conferences, but had never before given an interview.

'I am amazed and proud to be here, and I'm learning all the time. As soon as I signed for the team they sent a steering wheel round to my house so I could learn all the controls & the sequences for the start. I just kept it in my lap. When I got to the first race, I wasn't nervous about the start, because I knew everything'. McLaren made sure Hamilton was physically prepared and it was hard to imagine anyone looking fitter. Countless trips to the gym ensured that he'd develop the strength & stamina to cope with the rigours of racing an F1 car for up to 2 hrs in extreme heat.

'It was extremely exciting to do all the training. There was a point where we were doing all the same things over and over again, but then we started changing things & it became exciting again. You wouldn't believe what it's like in the car, the forces that are on you. I finish every race with a black ...a darker line down my side where I've been pushed against the seat, but the race is the most exciting part, the 1st corner, the first pit stop. I'm just going to get stronger and stronger. I'm not yet at my best'.

Lewis lived with his mum from the age of 2 'til he was 10, before moving in with his dad & stepmother Linda. A day out with his dad when 8 years old to Rye House kart track, a few miles south of Stevenage, changed his life. He'd already been karting, being a natural, soon lapping his dad Anthony, but he'd then decided that racing was what he wanted to do. A deal was struck between father and son: if Lewis worked hard at school, his dad would support his son's karting.

Anthony was working as an IT manager as Lewis began making a name for himself on the kart circuit. Taking time off became a problem as his son's racing & testing took him all over the country and overseas., so Anthony took redundancy so he could spend more time at the track. He did contract work & was sometimes doing 2 or 3 jobs at a time. He then set up his own computer company, which grew to employ 25 people, but his main role in life was working as his son's manager on a daily basis.

'If I didn't love it, I'm sure I wouldn't be as good as I am today, because I'd have put half the effort in and just have driven the races. I think you find drivers who just rely on their racing ability but don't do the hard yards. When you're young you don't really understand that philosophy: work hard then see the results. You think, "I can't be bothered to work hard now", & when you get there you struggle and complain, but if you really put the effort in you see the results. Even if you don't do well you know you've done the work, so next time you can improve on it', Lewis said.

As soon as he started competing, the results were spectacular. Adam Jones, a journalist & ex-racer who ran 100ccPR, an agency that dealt in public relations for kart racers, remembered meeting Hamilton in 1994. 'Martin Howell, who owned the Playscape indoor kart track in Clapham, introduced us. He said, "Adam, this is Lewis - he's going to be a Formula One world champion". I shook his hand then said, "You're going to be a Grand-Prix champion, eh?" and Lewis looked at me then said, "Yes, I am". I thought, "Yeah, right". What struck me wasn't Lewis's steely determination but Martin's tone. He wasn't patronising Lewis or me; he meant what he said. Every magazine or newspaper article about Lewis mentions his karting background, but what they fail to say is just how good he was back in those days. Lewis hasn't just suddenly arrived; he's been around a long time'.

Michael Eboda, editor of the New Nation, a newspaper aimed at Britain's black community, recalled arriving at Buckmore Park kart track in Kent to interview Hamilton & his dad for The Observer during 1997. 'I got there then asked someone where I could find Lewis Hamilton. They said, "He's the only black kid here, he'll be c. 3 laps ahead of everyone else". He was'. Eboda remembered the 12-year-old Hamilton as being polite and assured as they chatted in the back of a beaten-up old Peugeot hire car. He didn't want his dad with him as they talked, but Michael was more than a little surprised by the answer when he asked how Lewis drove a kart so fast. 'I don't know why I'm so quick. 'When I come to a corner the answer just comes. I take what the answer says & it makes me take it as quickly as possible'.

He'd always gone as quickly as possible. Kieran Crawley, head of M-Sport, one of Britain's leading kart teams, worked with the Hamiltons as Lewis made his way up through the karting levels. He recalled a race in Belgium, when Lewis was competing in the Junior Intercontinental A class, that showed just how quick he could be. 'Lewis was always stalling the kart, but you were allowed to wait by the side of the track with an engine starter. As they rolled on to the grid I could see Lewis looking for me. I thought, "Oh no, he's stalled it".

I got the starter into the side pod just as the lights went to green. Lewis went off from the back of the grid and was already half a lap down. He caught the pack then went through it to finish 4th. He was up against some very good drivers - including Robert Kubica, the Pole who's now a Formula 1 driver for BMW - & beat them. In Formula 1 we haven't seen him come from the back, but that's when he's at his most dangerous. When he makes mistakes, just watch him go. I want to see him make some mistakes - then you'll see just how good he is'.

Did Hamilton like the thought of charging through from the back after a mistake? It must happen 1 day soon in F1, as it had in Istanbul the previous year, in GP2, when he'd spun then worked his way up from 16th to 2nd: 'I rarely make mistakes in races. In Istanbul that was 1 of the few mistakes I've ever made'. Surely it was worth it? 'It was. It was great, but I was struggling in the car. The rear end was not right. Straight after that spin I somehow extracted a little bit more from the tyres and I had this boost & everything was right, the car was great and things need to be ...'Look at Kimi Raikkonen in Japan in 2005, when he came from the back. Everything was right, the car was fantastic and he got out of trouble when he did some of the most amazing moves you've ever seen. He was buzzing, he enjoyed it & he won. I love those experiences. I love coming from the back'.

Lewis' physical gifts extended beyond behind the wheel of a racing car. He took up karate after he attracted the attention of the school bully then by the age of 12, he was a black belt. He was also a very useful footballer at John Henry Newman School in Stevenage, having played in the same team there as Ashley Young, the England under-21 midfielder who joined Aston Villa from Watford during January '06 for £9.65m. 'I was quicker than Ashley Young, stronger than him, so I had that with me, but he was very skilled and very neat & would dribble the ball round people very nicely. I was very powerful in the team, I was always a midfielder and in my team I was the fittest by far, because of my racing & the training that I did. I'd run up and down & up and down & if someone tackled me I'd get them back. I'd always get them back, because I never gave up, whereas a lot of people would get tackled then just leave it for the next stage of the game. I'd never let that happen'.

Like all top sportsmen, Hamilton was very competitive, whether in a racing car or out 10-pin bowling with his mum. Did all the fun things in life involve keeping score? 'I think at a young age everything I did competitively I wanted to win, and I hated not being the best at any sport I did. When I competed against anyone I thought, "I've got to win", but I've got to a point now that I play golf & I lose, but I can deal with it. It's not a negative energy, I can control that energy'.

Did Lewis let his mum win at bowling? 'I don't ever let anyone win if I'm honest. I should let my brother win at some things, but it's very hard for me to do that'. He was referring to his 15 yr. old half-brother, Nicholas, who had cerebral palsy, the pair being extremely close. 'I always wanted a brother and I remember when my parents first told me they were going to have a boy, I was well excited. It's quite a cool feeling to watch someone grow up, to see the difficulties & troubles he's had, the experience he's had, to go through them with him and see how he pulls out of them.

I think he's just an amazing lad & I really love to do things for him. This weekend we're going racing remote-controlled cars. We bought him a new one then I bought one so we can race together. I've been a couple of times and I get hassled a little bit now, but I had my dad to take me & he doesn't have time, so when I do have time I love to just take my brother down to the track. He likes a challenge and he's got a lot steeper challenges'.

The future for Hamilton had huge possibilities, no doubt he'd win many Grands Prix & world drivers' championships, perhaps even more than the 7 titles that Michael Schumacher lifted before he retired at the end of 2006. He'd very soon be incredibly rich, although his salary was apparently 'just' £500,000 / season, 1/20th of team-mate Fernando Alonso's. Dominic Curran, a director of Karen Earl Sponsorship, believed Lewis had the potential to earn £100s of millions: 'He's arrived with about as big a bang as possible. He's got something different - he's the 1st black Formula One driver - which opens up a whole new market for him. Plus, he has charisma and star quality, he's a good-looking guy who speaks well, which is attractive to sponsors & he's clean-cut'.

What did Hamilton think of all that? How did he see himself in the future? 'I think when I'm done I'd just like to go back to living a normal life, have a family and no worries. Just enjoy doing things with my brother. There's a lot of experiences in life which I haven't had yet, and doing that with him & doing that with my friends and not having the worries, just enjoying. It's such an important thing'.

How did Lewis think he managed to be so calm & grounded? 'It comes from my parents, and being taught to appreciate things. I was like every kid. You get in trouble ... I liked living life on the edge but I was always taught to appreciate things & say "Thank you". I got that from my dad but also from my mum. A lot of my personality comes from my mum. It's a real half and half'.

At McLaren there was nothing but praise for their record-breaking recruit. 'I could launch into a whole range of eulogies. You just need to look at the history of Formula 1 to see how his debut compares. How could anyone expect a start like this? It's not just what he does on the track but it's what he says & how he says it. You have the impression that here is a guy who'll keep his feet on the ground. He has enough Brownie points to avoid criticism if something goes wrong - which it will. It's inevitable for any driver, but you have the feeling that Lewis will be able to cope with that too', said Ron Dennis.

The team's chief executive, Martin Whitmarsh, knew exactly just how good Hamilton was. 'Since I joined McLaren in 1989, I've worked with a lot of great drivers, including Alain Prost, Ayrton Senna, Mika Hakkinen and now Fernando Alonso. It's pretty clear that Lewis ticks all the necessary boxes. It's too early to analyse, but if the trend continues there's no reason why he couldn't become the greatest driver ever'. Hamilton's influence was extending far beyond the insular world of F1. Michael Eboda, of New Nation, could already see the impact that he was having on black Britons. 'He's incredibly popular & he's a fantastic role model, as is his dad. It sends out a message to folk that that's the way to bring up a kid'.

McLaren were extremely protective of their new star, in a similar way to how Alex Ferguson had once chaperoned the young Ryan Giggs at Man. Utd. One couldn't ask Lewis about race and ethnicity or whether he intended, like most Formula One drivers, to become a tax exile. At the Spanish Grand Prix the previous month Hamilton had mentioned that he might one day have to move to Switzerland for tax reasons, but his dad rapidly killed the story.

McLaren needn't have worried, because Lewis wouldn't let the team down. He hadn't been fazed by what he'd achieved so far in his career, let alone in Formula One, where he'd placed the big stars, including his team-mate Fernando Alonso, under intense pressure. The Lewis Hamilton story was much nearer its start than its end, with the world still waking up to just what was possible.

Was that what worried McLaren, that they thought their big new star might start to feel & act like one? 'I've never read about something I've said, because I know what I've said. My parents might say, "There's a good piece in the paper, do you want to read it?", but I won't read it. It's a good way of keeping your feet on the ground, because when you read stuff like that you think, "Wow! It's great!" and you feel yourself floating. As I don't read the stuff about me, I don't feel like a superstar. I don't understand folk who do have that mentality, "I'm a superstar!" It's just a job. It's a fantastic job & people just perceive you for some reason as a superstar, but at the end of the day I'm just Lewis. I've always been Lewis, and it's important to me to stay like that, because folk will take me like that'.

As Lewis Hamilton rose through the ranks of competitive go-karting, his dad, Anthony, told him: "Always do your talking on the track". Hamilton had a lot to talk about. Bullying & racial taunts were a consistent feature of his childhood in Stevenage, Hertfordshire, a new town 30 miles north of London; his dad taught him the best response was to excel at his sport. The trouble was that he didn't have many folk to talk to about what he was going through. Lewis is mixed-race, the son of a white mother, Carmen Larbalestier, who brought him up until he was 12, when he went to live with his Grenadian-British father, from whom she'd separated when he was 2:

"My mum was wonderful. She was so loving, but she didn't fully understand the impact of the things I was experiencing at school. The bullying and being picked on, while my dad was quite tough, so I didn't tell him too much about those experiences. As a kid I remember just staying quiet about it, because I didn't feel anyone really understood. I just kept it to myself. I took up boxing because I needed to channel the pain. I learned karate because I was being beaten up & I wanted to be able to defend myself".

As close to London as Stevenage is, it might as well have been in a different universe. In London the Black experience seemed authentic, but in Stevenage it felt synthetic. Race in London was something you read about in the papers, while race in Stevenage was something that wasn't even acknowledged. Racing was a release for Hamilton, who became the town's most famous son. "I got in a car where I was the only kid of colour on the track, so I'd be getting pushed around, but then I could always turn their energy against them. I'd out-trick them, outsmart them, outwit them and beat them, which for me was more powerful than any words".

Lewis was on Zoom, sitting in front of a huge TV, on a massive sofa, in the motor-home that he used for European races, parked on site at Circuit Paul Ricard in Le Castellet, ahead of the French Grand Prix. His oval, caramel-coloured face was framed by well-groomed facial hair, with his plaits poking out from the back of his head. He chatted in an unguarded, reflective manner, without guile or jargon, gesturing with his hands, while occasionally smiling.

On the track Hamilton talked with the greatest of authority. Aged 36, he was probably the most accomplished Formula 1 driver of all time, with 98 grand prix wins, 100 pole positions & 171 podium finishes. The only significant record that he hadn't broken was that of the number of drivers' championships won, being tied with Michael Schumacher at 7 but many believed him to be the best ever seen, still being at the top of his game.

Over the past year, off the track Lewis had begun to find his voice regarding his racial identity; taking a knee; raising a clenched fist, as long dormant concerns over racism and discrimination had been awakened following the Black Lives Matter uprisings. Hamilton had transformed from a compliant, go-with-the-flow character to a change agent who was determined to make waves. He'd shaped the way others saw him, from an inoffensive, if gaffe-prone, socialite focused only on his sport, to a politically aware role model conscious of his wider cultural significance. He was about to take on the sport that had brought him fame & fortune, with a commission demanding racial diversity and significant outreach to under represented groups, as well as more racial equality.

It had been a long journey for Lewis, with some been bumps along the road. "I'd be in Newcastle when folk would shout, 'Go back to your country,' or in Spain during 2008, when people painted themselves black & put on wigs, really mocking my family, and I remember the sport not saying anything about it". After stewards penalised him for a couple of collisions in Monaco in 2011, he was asked: 'Why are you such a magnet for stewards? You obviously feel that you're being targeted'. Hamilton replied: "Maybe it's because I'm Black. That's what Ali G says, I don't know". The Telegraph ran a headline: 'Lewis risks disciplinary action after astonishing outburst'.

"It often felt that maybe I didn't speak about race in the right way, or wasn't great at explaining it, or maybe educated enough to talk about it. Either way, I got a lot of push-back, it seemed like more hassle than it was worth, so I reverted to just doing my talking on the track", Hamilton said. If he'd anything to say, he'd do so privately. He remembered returning from the British Cadet Karting Championship in 1995, aged 10, singing Queen's We Are The Champions in the camper van with his dad. "No one saw it. We didn't do it in folk's faces. We had so much against us".

His attitude changed during 2020, when before the Austrian Grand Prix, just a month after George Floyd's murder, F1's only black driver donned a Black Lives Matter T-shirt, taking the knee. When some drivers declined to follow Lewis' lead, he told them that "Silence is complicit", before they all donned End Racism T-shirts, with 14 drivers joining him in kneeling, while 6 stood behind them. The following week, after he won the Styrian Grand Prix, also in Austria, he raised his fist in a Black power salute.

Hamilton also called out his competitors with a social media post: 'I see those of you who're staying silent, some of you the biggest stars, yet you stay silent in the midst of injustice', before gunning for Formula One as a whole: "It's lacking leadership. It shouldn't be for me to have to call the teams or call the teams out". At the same race, Formula 1, which controls the cameras broadcasting the event, cut away from the moment when some of the drivers took the knee, instead showing Red Bull skydivers dropping from the sky.

"This wrath of emotions came up & I couldn't contain myself. I was in tears, this stuff came up that I'd suppressed over all those years, which was so powerful, sad but also releasing, and I thought, 'I can't stay quiet. I need to speak out, because there are folk experiencing what I'm experiencing, or 10 times worse, or 100 times worse. They need me right now', so when I did speak out that was me letting the black community know: 'I hear you & I stand with you'", stated Lewis.

However, one got the impression that although Hamilton might have thought about it a lot, he still hadn't spoken about it much. He wasn't reciting well-rehearsed lines; his words carried the air of a confession, which sounded like a lot to take on. "I don't see it as a burden. It was definitely liberating to be able to be open and speak about things. For folk to know that there's much more to me than perhaps they realised from watching me on TV. I feel like I was built for this. There's a reason it was suppressed over all that time and if it had happened any sooner I wouldn't have been ready, wouldn't have been strong enough to handle it. I wouldn't be able to do my job as well while doing both things at the same time, but now I'm equipped with the tools to do so. I look at my niece & nephew. I look at my little cousins then I think, 'How can I make things better for you guys and your friends?'"

While the outrage & activism that followed George Floyd's murder gave Lewis the confidence to speak up, Black Lives Matter didn't create his racial consciousness: it emboldened it. He had in the past cited Nelson Mandela, Martin Luther King and his own dad as his role models, with Bob Marley, Nas & Marvin Gaye being among his favourite musicians. He knew that his racial difference meant something. "Being Black isn't a negative, it's a positive if anything, because I'm different. In the future that can open doors to different cultures... showing that not only white folk can do it... It'll be good to mean something", Hamilton said in 2007, who just hadn't worked out what that meaning was, what to make of it or what to do about it.

He'd already asked himself why there were so few members of colour on his team, without getting satisfactory answers. Mercedes revealed during the summer of 2020 that 3% of its F1 staff were from ethnic minorities, but of over 40,000 jobs in motor-sport in the UK, under 1% were filled by people from black backgrounds. Lewis worked with the Royal Academy of Engineering in 2019 to undertake some research, hoping to improving the representation of black folk in motor sport. "We had no idea that the whole George Floyd situation would kick in" he said, as The Black Lives Matter movement give the initiative a sense of urgency and broader relevance.

The resulting Hamilton Commission was published on 13th July '21, having embraced a broad agenda including school exclusions, Lewis having been excluded after a fellow pupil was attacked, needing treatment in hospital, before being reinstated when it was shown that he was wrongly identified as being involved. It also covered anti-racist curriculums, while actively promoting science, technology, engineering & mathematics to students of colour, having examined targeted programmes for graduates and those in post-16 education from diverse backgrounds & expanded motor-sport apprenticeships. Its board had a broad pool of expertise and disciplines, including a Labour & Tory MP, a Formula One grandee, a trade unionist, professors, engineers and equality campaigners.

For Lewis, who'd been actively involved in the commission's process, the mission was deeply personal: "Over time, I've been trying to figure out my purpose. There's got to be a reason that I'm not only the only black driver but the one at the front & it's not just about winning. I won the world championship last year and in that year everything became visible, I felt that my purpose was shown to me & now I'm on that journey".

As the Black Lives Matter demonstrations were getting bigger during 2020, Ben Carrington, an associate professor of sociology and journalism at USC Annenberg, sat in on an informal on-line gathering of one of the leading Formula 1 teams. He stated that he asked one of the team's most senior figures what he thought of Hamilton's stance, being stunned at the response: "Well, if Lewis is really so committed to that cause, perhaps he should donate all of his salary to it", the boss said, before going on to say that his team was so non-racial that he didn't know how many Black or Asian employees there were, because he didn't "see race".

"He seemed to be insinuating that Lewis' beliefs weren't sincere, with his wealth somehow undermining his stance. It was such a tone-deaf, arrogant response, that it would almost certainly have got that person fired if they were in the NBA or NFL, but it made me realise, Wow! This is what Hamilton is up against within F1", said Carrington, author of Race, Sport And Politics: The Sporting Black Diaspora.

In such an exclusive sport, racial discrimination is invariably linked to class, Lewis' dad having had to re-mortgage his house & spend all his and his 2nd wife's savings to get his son through just one year of go-karting, who was the lucky one among his peers: "We had dear friends who threw everything & the kitchen sink at it, but today don't have any money," Hamilton said. The young Lewis found an advocate in Ron Dennis, head of the McLaren team,who he approached when he was 10, wearing a borrowed silk suit, telling Ron that he wanted to drive for him. Dennis replied, in Hamilton's autograph book: "Try me in 9 years".

By the age of 13, Lewis had joined McLaren's young driver programme then by 22 he'd made his Formula One debut as a McLaren driver, going on to win the world championship in his 2nd season in 2008. Ron had referred to Hamilton as his 'My Fair Lady project', telling Sky News: 'Our relationship was very much positioned as surrogate father and son – I don't think Anthony would have ever been uncomfortable with that".

Lewis has called Formula 1 a "Billionaire boys' club. There's no way that we'd make it now if we started from where we started". He believed that was one of the things that had driven his success. "I know how hard it was for my dad just to have fresh tyres at the weekend. It's impacted me heavily. I can't just think, 'I deserve to be here'. I can't squander this opportunity. I have to grab it with both hands & really dig deep every single time I'm in the car".

Others had it far easier. Hamilton was runner-up at the French Grand Prix behind Max Verstappen, whose dad was F1 driver Jos; 3rd being Sergio Pérez, whose dad was a driver and agent, having been sponsored from an early age by the son of billionaire Carlos Slim, formerly the world's richest man. 5th was Lando Norris, whose dad had a fortune of £200m. The only other driver in the top 5 with a modest background was Lewis' Mercedes team-mate Valtteri Bottas, whose dad owned a small cleaning company, with his mum being an undertaker. However, he wasn't primarily interested in opportunities for racing drivers: "There are only 20 seats in the drivers' space. That's not so important to me, but there are over 40,000 jobs across motor-sports in the UK, with less than 1% being filled by folk from Black backgrounds, so there are a lot of opportunities in many different categories, not just engineering".

The Hamilton Commission's recommendations were ambitious & logical. They included asking Formula One teams to implement a diversity charter; increasing the number of Black teachers in science, technology, engineering & mathematics [Stem] subjects; a fund to expose excluded students to Stem and motor-sport-related activities & a scholarship programme to encourage Black Stem graduates into specialist motor sport roles. However, the world wasn't short of commissions providing proposals on how to further equality in a range of areas. The challenge was getting institutions to adopt the plans as their own, prioritising then enforcing them. "I want this to be about action. I know there's a lot of commissions that perhaps don't get the backing or manage to continue, but this one has me, and I don't fail at a lot of things", said Lewis.

Formula 1 isn't for everyone, some folk being compelled by strategic tyre changes, fast straights & tight corners, while others are indifferent to the sight of cars whizzing around for hours on end. However, Hamilton's dominance spoke for itself, British sporting figures rarely attaining his level of global supremacy, so it was strange that he'd never had the great national acclaim of others, who'd achieved far less in their fields.

A YouGov poll during October 2020, the year that he'd equalled Michael Schumacher's championship-winning record, found that only 21% of Britons thought Lewis deserved a knighthood, compared with 46% who said he didn't, although he was given one in the New Year honours of 2021. In a YouGov poll of the most popular all-time sports personalities, he came 37th, well behind Michael Schumacher (9th) and the late Stirling Moss, who never won a world drivers' championship (15th).

Why didn't folk like Hamilton more? "I'm not living my life to make everyone happy. You can't make everyone happy. People are always going to have their own opinions". He thought it might be due to his many gaffes: taking a selfie while riding a Harley-Davidson in New Zealand, reckless driving incidents off the track & the time that he'd directly sprayed a woman on the podium with champagne. Lewis also referred to Stevenage as 'the slums', and made jokes about his nephew's princess dress on social media telling him: "Boys don't wear princess dresses".

He fired his own dad as his manager in 2010, although compared with other celebrity parent/manager splits, it seemed to be relatively civilised & cordial: the inevitable, if painful, disentanglement of work and family that comes with maturity, but at the time the media made it out to be a callous act of betrayal. The pair had since reconciled, with his dad being back on the team but there was also the challenge of aligning his lifestyle with his pronouncements. Anti-racist messages were easier to dismiss when they came from a tax haven in Monaco, where he lived; statements about climate change from the top driver of a sport that produced so much carbon emissions could also seem hypocritical.

Hamilton had apologised for most of his missteps, turned vegan, sold his private jet & insisted that his Tommy Hilfiger clothing line was sustainable, having become a strident voice for improving environmental standards in F1. However, criticisms seemed to stick to him in a way that they didn't to others. "I haven't done things in a perfect way. I was never media trained. I was just thrown into a room with folk, while at the same time I'm probably a later bloomer, growing into my adulthood, because I'd been this kid protected by my dad for a long time then suddenly I'm really in a man's world and I'm being asked all these questions. Everything I say is taken literally, all the mistakes are in plain sight".

This helped explained Lewis' support for tennis champion Naomi Osaka after she pulled out of the French Open following a dispute with organisers about her refusal to speak to journalists, praising her bravery: "It's not that I have an opinion about everything, but I know what it's like to be young in sport. I didn't have strong enough shoulders to do what she's done at her age, so I'm proud of her. I wish my young self had me to say, 'You're going to be good'. I had my dad, but even for him it was all new".

There was more to Hamilton's less favoured status than that though, as he lacked a solid constituency beyond Formula One fans, being difficult to place. The political voice of anti-racist protest that he was nurturing had a long lineage from Muhammad Ali to Colin Kaepernick, but the influences on his literal voice were difficult to fathom, his accent being a kind of intercontinental, media-enunciated, home counties hybrid that defied categorisation.

Lewis was a very wealthy biracial man from a working-class background in an elite sport, from a town with which very few Britons had any cultural association. He had character, but he wasn't a character. We'd never seen or heard his like before. Shonda Rhimes, the TV producer of Grey's Anatomy, Scandal & Bridgerton, referred in her autobiography, The Year Of Yes, to a FOD – first, only and different. "When you're an FOD you're saddled with that burden of extra responsibility, whether you want it or not. This wasn't just my shot. It was ours".

Watching Hamilton during 2007, when he was seriously contending for the drivers' championship in his 1st season, Kieron Rablah, who was also brought up in Stevenage related: "When I see him on TV I just can't help cheering. I'd not watched a Formula One race for 10 years, but all I keep thinking when I see him racing is: he's a Black kid from Stevenage. It's not just that he's made it to that level, which would be pretty amazing in any sport; it's that he's made it in Formula 1. If you come from Stevenage, F1 might as well be polo".

Feeling comfortable in one's own skin was easier said than done under those conditions. "I remember not being able to be myself, of not being able to speak the way I wanted to speak. That's the point of all this inclusivity: including people, not asking them to change in order to fit. I remember feeling that I had to be a different shape. The entry point to my sport was a square but I was like a hexagon, so I thought, 'I'm never going to fit through that bloody thing'. I had to morph my way in, in order to fit into that world then try to get back into the shape I was before", said Lewis.

Even as he competed for a record 8th world championship, his sights were set both on the horizon & in the rear-view mirror at his legacy. "My dream when I was younger was to get to Formula One then I thought I'd love to emulate Ayrton Senna then I reached 3 world championships [Senna's record before he died] then I'm like, shoot, now what? My dream now is to be a father like my dad one day, but better. Just as he wanted to be like his dad one day, but a better version of his dad. I want to carry on the Hamilton name and make him proud".

Was there something that he wanted to reveal? "No, no, no, no! I'm not there yet". Although single, he'd been linked to many models & singers over the years, from Rita Ora to Nicole Scherzinger. The athlete John Carlos once said that when he'd raised his fist on the podium at the Mexico City Olympics of 1968, the first thing he'd thought was: 'The shackles have been broken and they won't ever be able to put shackles on John Carlos again, because what had been done couldn't be taken back... The greatest problem is that we're afraid to offend our oppressors'.

There was no going back for Lewis. The shackles had been broken, but there was more to freedom than just the breaking of chains. Isolated in his sport, nurturing his voice in public even as he continued his talking on the track, the path forward promised to be as personally fulfilling as it was politically perilous. "We'll see where we can go. As the years pass, you realise that success is a wonderful thing, but it feels relatively short-lived & I don't just want to be remembered as a driver, because I care about so many more different things".

Formula 1 World Champion Michael Schumacher had tipped British karting sensation Lewis Hamilton for future F1 success, after the pair took part in the World Karting Championship event, held at Kerpen one weekend in October 2001. Michael, who was making a guest appearance in the series at his dad Rolf's circuit, said that the youngster had got what it took to make it to the top, complimenting the driver's talent and commitment: "He's a quality driver, very strong and only 16. If he keeps this up I'm sure that he'll reach F1. It's something special to see a kid of his age out on the circuit. He's clearly got the right racing mentality".

Hamilton made history when he became the 1st Briton to win the European Karting Championship, at the age of 15, having begun racing when he was 8, already being regarded as one of the most successful kart racers in the World. Lewis had been signed by McLaren-Mercedes for a long term contract, with the Woking based team funding his karting career. McLaren chief Ron Dennis was also his personal manager. If Hamilton made it into Formula One, he also stood a good chance of becoming the first black driver to take part in the World Championship since its inception.

Years in the future folk might look back on Michael Schumacher's retirement, saying, 'If only he'd raced for one more year – then we would've seen him compete with Lewis Hamilton'. Lewis had a long way to go to become a great of Schumacher's stature, but his performances during his debut season had been very impressive, leading the championship with 3 rounds to go. They might never be destined to meet on a Formula 1 track, but they'd raced once before, when a 16 year-old Lewis took on Michael in karts during October 2001.

A famous TV advert for a sportswear company several years earlier had featured top footballers having a kick-about with scores of amateur players on Hackney Marshes in London, but how often did professional sportsmen do the same thing in real life? Well, Michael Schumacher had in 2001. Just after winning his 4th World Championship he flew back from the final round at Suzuka in Japan then headed straight for the gym, as he needed to trim 3 KG from his already slender frame to be competitive in a World Karting Championship final that was being held at his dad Rolf's circuit in Kerpen. "I am of course aware that these guys against whom I'll be racing, drive every day, while I maybe do only 3 times / year, but that entices me even more," Michael said.

Hamilton, aged 16, was at a pivotal point in his career, having already got the backing of McLaren several years earlier, being poised to make the switch from karting to racing cars. He'd begun testing for Manor Motor-sport in preparation for that winter's British Formula Renault series. Lewis would be leaving a fine pedigree in karting behind, having won the European Formula A championship during the year 2000 then the Formula A World Cup that same year.

In the last practice session before the sequence of heats & finals got under-way, Schumacher was quickest of all, setting a new lap record for the circuit with a time of 43.956 secs. However, qualifying on the Saturday brought a change of fortune for the German, as the drivers were split into 2 groups with Michael's session being hit by rain, leaving him 22nd. That afternoon Schumacher and Lewis were in the same race together, the Briton finishing runner-up to Vitantonio Liuzzi. Michael climbed through the field to finish 8th, having been as high as 6th, ending the race 9.5 secs behind the winner.

In the 2nd heat that Sunday Schumacher & Hamilton finished in the opposite order, Michael coming 15th, with Lewis trailing in 26th, which meant that they'd start the 1st of the finals from 16th and 26th respectively. The first final began well for Schumacher as he moved up the field to take 3rd place, but on lap 15 he seemed to brake too deep into a tight corner, spinning the kart & stalling the engine, with several attempts to restart it failing, leaving him in 25th overall. In stark contrast, Hamilton rose from 26th on the grid to finish 7th.

Michael made a good start in the final race , climbing to 7th place by the end of the 1st lap, having passed Hamilton's team-mate Nico Rosberg, who latched onto the back of Schumacher's kart then followed his experienced compatriot as he rose up through the field. By just under half race distance, on lap 11, Michael was up to 4th with Nico 6th and Lewis back in 9th. The race leader Franck Perera & 2nd placed Maro Ardigo clashed, leaving a furious Franck in the gravel being restrained by a marshal.

Maro won with Schumacher coming in 3rd but after Ardi was disqualified the German was promoted to runner-up behind Sauro Cesetti, with Rosberg 3rd and Hamilton 7th. Asked about the race afterwards, Lewis replied with the kind of nonplussed coolness folk had come to associate with him: "I never really had a chance to get near Schumacher, which was a shame, because I'd have liked to have beaten him around a few corners. I could see him in the distance in the 2nd race, but to be fair it didn't really make much of a difference to me".

Liuzzi won the World Karting Championship that year before becoming Formula 3000 champion in 2004 then making his F1 debut with Red Bull. Nico lifted the GP2 championship trophy of 2005 then started Formula One with the Williams team the following year. Estonian Marko Asmer, 4th in the final race, won the British Formula Three championship then targeted a move to Formula 1, while Giedo van der Garde, who retired on the 7th lap, was McLaren's 'other' development driver, also being one of Spyker's 4 test drivers, while being well down in the World Series by Renault.

The 10-yr-old schoolboy who approached McLaren's team chief, Ron Dennis, at an awards ceremony stuck out his hand then said politely, "Hello, my name is Lewis Hamilton & one day I'd like to drive for McLaren". A week later, having checked out the youth's credentials, Ron called Lewis' dad Anthony, who'd suggested that there was nothing to lose by introducing himself to Dennis, offering to underwrite his son's racing career.

Ron had just made Hamilton's teenage dream come true by confirming that the 21-year-old from Tewin, in Hertfordshire, would drive for the revamped McLaren-Mercedes team for the Formula One world championship of 2007, alongside the title holder, Fernando Alonso. Lewis said "It's a dream come true. To be racing in Formula 1 with McLaren has been the ultimate goal since I was very young and this opportunity is a fantastic way to end what has been the best year. I've grown up with McLaren & Mercedes and wouldn't be where I am today without their support & guidance. I'm aware that this will be a challenge and I know that there'll be a lot of attention on me, but the team have told me to relax, do the best I can & enjoy the opportunity. I'll work hard to get results".

Hamilton had been a part of the McLaren and Mercedes-Benz Young Driver Support Programme since its inception during 1998, and with Dennis' backing he won the McLaren-Mercedes Champions of the Future kart series before going on to triumph in 10 of the 15 races of the British Formula Renault Championship in 2003. A couple of years later he dominated the Formula Three Euro Series in his 2nd season, before winning the GP2 championship of 2006 in style at his 1st attempt with 5 victories.

Opinion had been divided over whether going up against a driver of Fernando's calibre was a wise move in his rookie season, but Lewis said he had no qualms on that score & Ron stated that he had complete faith in his protégé. "I'm distinctly unimpressed by the majority of drivers in F1. Lewis is well equipped to deal with the drivers who fall into that category. Of course we have reservations; Lewis is an unproven product, but having the world champion in one of our cars means that we can be less conservative and take the opportunity to give Lewis his chance".

Hamilton was given the news of his graduation on 30th Sept. '06, but it wasn't made public then to let the outcome of the world championship be decided & the news of Michael Schumacher's retirement sink in. Dennis said that it was the right time, as testing was recommencing in Barcelona the following week to signal the start of all the teams' campaigns of 2007. Pedro de la Rosa, who stood in 2006 when Juan Pablo Montoya left the team, would revert to test driver status, together with Briton Gary Paffett.

Lewis, who broke new ground as the first black driver to race in Formula One, was highly regarded within the sport, not least by Ron, who paid tribute to his dad Anthony and step-mother Linda. "Lewis gets his basic character from his family values & we've just supplemented them. He was a well rounded individual who appreciates not just what McLaren-Mercedes have done for him, but also what his family have done for him".

The first black driver named to race in Formula 1 during 2007 had a Caribbean background; 21 year old Brit Lewis Hamilton, partnering the reigning world champion Fernando Alonzo at MacLaren that season, having Grenadian roots, with his paternal grandparents being from the Caribbean Spice Isle.

Comparisons with Tiger Woods had been made, as like Woods, Hamilton Jnr. was a marketing-man's dream; young, articulate and good-looking, being expected to attract a new demographic to the white, middle-class world of F1. The tale of his rise could've been taken straight from a Hollywood script, the usually unsentimental McLaren-Mercedes boss Ron Dennis having said that it had the "attraction of being a bit of a My Fair Lady story".

The pair had 1st met at an awards ceremony in London during 1995, when the 10-year-old Lewis made a big impression on the McLaren supremo: "When I first met Lewis he was asking for my autograph. Unlike so many folk, he looked me square in the face when informing me where he was going in his life. Without breaking eye contact, he told me how he was going to go about his career. It impressed the hell out of me", said Dennis.

He remembered the meeting then signed Hamilton up to the McLaren development programme a couple of years later, his rise since then having been inexorable. Lewis won the British Formula Renault series of 2003, the Formula 3 Euroseries in 2005 then the GP2 title the following year. Ron said that he'd been been a model pupil: "Confidence is often coupled with arrogance, but there isn't an ounce of arrogance in Lewis. He listened, which so frequently young people don't then progressively built his career. He's deserved this opportunity".

Stories about Hamilton had often focused on the driver's ethnicity but Dennis insisted that it had never been a consideration for him: "To be honest, it just doesn't register & never has. We're very aware of the ability of Lewis' colour to be used as a headline, but for us, it's just immaterial. We don't hide from the fact that he's from a mixed-race background, but it just doesn't matter. The Tiger Woods label makes you smile and you could argue it's a compliment, but it's just not relevant to our objectives. He's in the team because he's earned it, not because of his colour".

Hamilton must've been tired of being asked questions about his race, but he embraced the chance to become a role-model for ethnic groups wanting to enter Formula One: "Hopefully it can encourage other ethnic groups to get involved in the sport. It doesn't have to be just for one group of people, it can be for everyone. Hopefully when I'm there folk that can relate to me will see that it s possible, so also try to get into the sport".

Not only would Lewis have to contend with the label of the 'Tiger Woods of Formula 1' but also the prospect of being compared in equal equipment to the best driver in the sport. F1 was an unforgiving world at the best of times, let alone when one was the team-mate of the youngest double champion in history but the 21-year-old from Stevenage said he was looking forward to working with Alonso: "I view it as a positive. I think I can benefit from having such a strong team-mate and I'm looking forward to working with him. I'm going to try to do the best job I can, learn from him as quickly as possible and eventually compete against him".

Ron said that already having such a strong driver in the team would give Hamilton space to develop, believing that the youngster could win a race that coming season. "Having an expectation of Lewis winning next season isn't unrealistic, as long as we have a strong car, but certainly not in the early part of the season. If he's not too hyped he can blossom as a Grand Prix driver".

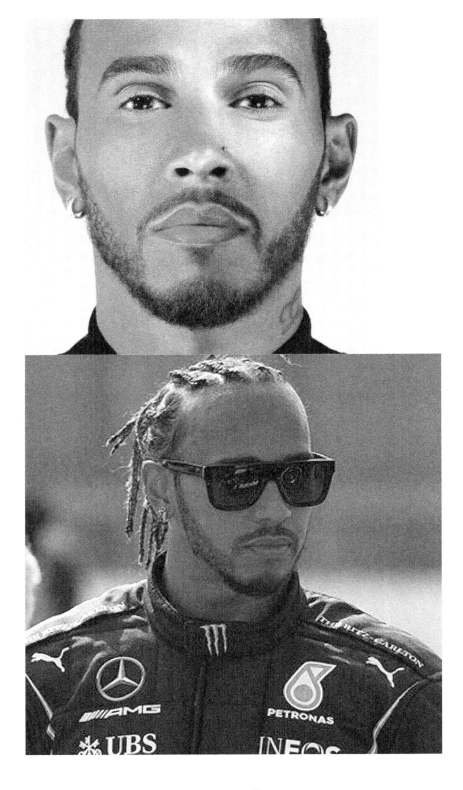

Printed in Great Britain
by Amazon